THE PREGNANT UNICORN

THE PREGNANT UNICORN

by

CHRISTOPHER PORTWAY

Foreword by Lord Brockway

TERENCE DALTON LIMITED

LAVENHAM · SUFFOLK

1969

Published by
TERENCE DALTON LIMITED
S B N 900963 12 3

Jacket Design by
ALAN WRIGHT

Photo Engravings by
STAR ILLUSTRATION WORKS LIMITED

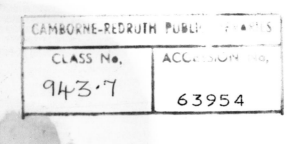
Printed in Great Britain at

THE LAVENHAM PRESS LIMITED

LAVENHAM   SUFFOLK

CONTENTS

To Jarka Anna and those who helped.

Acknowledgements

Acknowledgements are due to George Allen & Unwin Ltd. for allowing reproduction of paragraphs of "Outside the Right" by Lord Brockway and also to William Blackwood & Sons Ltd. who first published a shortened version of the last three chapters of the story under the title of "Pregnant Unicorn" in Blackwood's Magazine, January 1968.

For much work on the typescript the author is heavily indebted to his wife together with Mrs. June Dalton and Mrs. Grace Hall.

FOREWORD

by

LORD BROCKWAY

I became involved in this story incidentally. From 1950 to 1964 I was member of Parliament for Eton and Slough, a strangely cosmopolitan constituency. Attracted by the industrial prosperity of Slough, it has recently received a large population of Commonwealth immigrants, but before then it was host to an unusual proportion of emigres from Europe, many from Communist countries. Thus I became concerned in uniting families across the frontiers; an aged father from Romania, a baby daughter from Czechoslovakia, a mother from Soviet Russia, two fiancees from Yugoslavia. Each case took months of negotiations, but at last there were emotional meetings at Heathrow.

Christopher Portway was not a constituent, but I was moved by his intensity of purpose when he came to see me. I found we differed profoundly about politics but that didn't matter. The human right to love is above any ideological conflict. But I confess I was confused, going to see Dr. Hajek, the Czech Ambassador, when he produced an earlier book by Christopher Portway telling of his adventures to meet and marry his first wife, also a Czech girl! It wasn't merely the repetitive coincidence but the fact that the book was bitterly anti-Communist, as this book is. I did not expect the heads of a Communist state to be sympathetic to the author.

But Dr. Hajek and I were old friends. He reminded me of a speech I had made at the Socialist International Conference in Vienna in 1928, warning the German Social Democrats of Hitler. I knew him to be a man of human sympathies and I did not despair. In fact, I know—this I did not reveal to Christopher Portway at the time, because it was understandably confidential—Jiri Hajek on successive occasions in Prague pressed his claims against stone-wall opposition. At last he won permission for Anna to come here.

Since then Jiri Hajek has become an international figure, not only revered by the Czech people, but admired by all who love freedom by his courageous opposition to the Soviet occupation of Czechoslovakia and his dedication to the principle of liberty. He himself has become the victim of authoritarian power, compelled to resign his Foreign Secretaryship because of the brave speech he delivered to the United Nations. His name will live in the annals of freedom.

9

This book is unique. It is a love story, but more. If it were only a story of enduring love it would be memorable. But to this is added the almost incredible story of Christopher's never given-up endeavours over five years to reach Anna over forbidden frontiers and to bring her to England. It is a record of an ingenuity and of an indominable spirit which proves again how fact can be more exciting and moving than fiction.

I was present at the marriage of Anna and Christopher and thought that was the end of my participation. But no. Having risked imprisonment for Anna he risked his life for her brother-in-law. I became involved in getting permission for Pavel to remain here but I am glad that I didn't know the whole truth about forged passports.

I have written that political differences never deter when human happiness is at stake, but in contributing this preface I must disassociate myself from the author's political attitude. I believe in personal freedom as deeply as anyone but I also believe in social justice and racial equality and neither west nor east has a clean record. The need to-day is co-existence. The need to-morrow is synthesis, uniting social justice and racial harmony with liberties of thought and movement.

With that qualification, I commend this book. I congratulate Christopher Portway on his writing, which sweeps one along with breathless excitement. It is an epic of the courage which love can inspire.

FENNER BROCKWAY

Introduction

In the arsenal of polite drawing room dialogue there is one question that never ceases to raise within me, if not embarrassment, then acute exasperation. It usually follows a pause in the small talk and a critical glance at the foreign books on the shelf or the framed pencil sketch of Prague's Hradcany Castle on the wall. One can almost see it coming.

"And where did you meet your wife?"

The question is usually couched in terms of polite indifference and in a tone of query which indicates that the enquirer could hardly care less. Or, anyway, that is how it seems to me.

There are, I have found, two ways of dealing with this question. One consists of the somewhat brutal counter question: "Which wife?" However, this invariably confuses the second party and not unnaturally antagonises my present wife to whom the subject of her predecessor is rightly taboo.

The second method is to launch straight into the long rigmarole of the mechanics of the affair. This safely by-passes the slippery slope of past affections but by no means explains the background. And the background is an important prop to the small drama that a proper reply to the question unfolds.

It is a long story.* It began in the last year of the war, 1945. Like a savage beast at bay Germany was fighting desperate battles for survival on all fronts. In the West the Anglo-American armies were already over the frontiers of the Fatherland itself. In the East the great sledgehammer of the Red Army was smashing at the defenders of the shrinking front lines in Poland, Silesia, Slovakia, Hungary. Behind these raging battles the greatest migration in history was spewing its vast rivers of human misery across the Silesian plain and into Czechoslovakia and Saxony. This story was born within the maelstrom of refugee and prisoner columns that choked the ice-bound roads to clash and merge with young Wehrmacht reinforcements moving eastwards, and broken soldiers, grey with exhaustion, struggling westwards. Its birth was one tiny spark of light that flickered for a moment within a vacuum of despair and hideous cruelty.

I was one of ten thousand British, Russian and Yugoslav prisoners dragging weary starving bodies along the hard, straight roads of Bohemia early in March 1945. The worst excesses of the barbaric

*See "Journey to Dana" (William Kimber) 1955 and "Forbidden Frontier" (William Kimber) 1962.

evacuation were over. Spring's magic was in the air, the snows had receded and we were in a country whose populace looked upon us with infinite compassion. In a more practical vein the food situation suddenly improved as the Germans saw a way out of the almost insurmountable supply problem. And as the Czech bread and soup began replenishing our wasted frames the spirit of revolt, that for two months had been suppressed by the basic will to survive, stirred again within men's hearts.

In the autumn of the previous year, together with a Scottish friend, I had escaped from my camp in Poland. We had lasted a fortnight during which by freight and passenger trains and on foot we had travelled sixty miles in the wrong direction, rectified this calamity and regained Cracow sixty miles in the right direction. Warsaw, half ringed by the Red Army, had been our ultimate objective. Our clandestine travels ended abruptly in Gestapo headquarters at Cracow and, following several days of their unpleasant attention in the cellars, we were returned to our *Stalag*. From then on we were given the honour of being labelled "dangerous characters" by our German guards and coal-mine working-camp overseers. But on that terrible winter march of 1944/45 our notoriety died. To escape in such conditions constituted certain death, our frozen bodies simply adding to the sickening trail of corpses that, like an avenue of stricken trees, marked that road of death for the first grim month.

We never gave our guards the opportunity of reasserting their "special measures" and, encouraged by a near miss with a bayonet jab when the haystack in which we lay hidden was thoroughly flushed, we partook of our second dose of freedom. We made our way to Prague, were bombed by American Flying Fortresses and, disgruntled, retired to the countryside. A vague idea of joining the Resistance governed our movements and when, near Kladno, we were taken under the wing of a farmer and his family it seemed our quest had ended. But the farmer had a daughter who, to a prisoner long suffering from a deficit of bread and sex, seemed utterly delectable. Dana was seventeen then and her ministering attentions soon cooled our ambitions to become heroes of the Underground. For a week we were pampered and fed and cleaned and just as we were becoming humans again the village Judas stepped in to betray us.

Back in a prisoner column, recently evacuated from a camp, we joined the war once more. I then found that, having taken so much from our Czech benefactors, I had left my heart behind in the little village of Kralovice. Time was to show that a welter of bombs and, later, shells, exclusively from our own side, a further escape, a candy-floss and SS suicide squad type war in company with the United States Third Army and finally the happiness of returning home could not retrieve the loss. For the first time in my life I was hopelessly in love.

My military career ended amongst the ruins and squalor of post-war Germany. In the British Army of the Rhine I landed the job of guarding German P.O.Ws including war criminals. The wheel of fortune had turned full circle but I evinced no great satisfaction. Dana and I corresponded regularly and I had been amazed and delighted to discover that my feelings for her were reciprocated. To me this was what really mattered.

I was no more success at business than I had been a soldier but life in the family seat at Great Maplestead, a charming little Essex village, had its compensations. The quiet, respectable existence washed away the scars and filth of war from my mind but a great dullness and loneliness became new emotions. With rumblings of paternal displeasure ringing in my ears I flew on St. Valentine's Day 1947 to Prague to confirm my engagement to Dana. I found both she and her village radiant with happiness at their new but, alas, short-lived freedom. An insignificant event at that time was a friendship I struck up with Dana's former schoolmaster and a series of visits to his school in the nearby town. These small incidents were, as we shall see, to become a vital cog in the machine that was grinding out my destiny.

A year later, in February 1948, politics—the violent politics of Communism—entered the story. The overthrow of President Benes, the murder of Czech Foreign Minister Jan Masaryk have passed into history, whilst the impenetrable "Iron Curtain", hallmark of the inhumanity of Stalin and his Soviet Empire, was extended to include the western frontiers of Czechoslovakia. Thus Communism won another bloodless but treacherous victory, and all countries east of a line from Luebeck, on the Baltic, to unsettled Greece fell silently into the harsh grip of a regime as ruthless as the one from which they had been so recently liberated.

Fortune still smiled upon me, however, for until the new Czech authority could get into its stride, there were loop-holes as yet unplugged in the closed frontier and late in April I again reached Prague. In May I married Dana beneath the threatening shadows of the hammer and sickle, and under banners proclaiming the mad rantings of President Gottwald and Joseph Stalin.

The marriage lasted no longer than the engagement. It was doomed from the start. I suppose our affection for one another had been built upon the cardboard base of a romantic vision. Foreign-soldier-returning-to-the-land-he-liberated-to-marry-girl-who-risked-her-life-for-him sort of thing. The newspapers had a ball. The hard realities and routine of normal life soon had the edifice crumbling.

But I was still blind to the inevitable when news came that my father-in-law was dying of cancer. Dana flew back to the land behind the curtain for a short visit. I saw her off from London Airport and arranged to meet her there ten days later. Then the great silence began. The days turned to weeks, and the weeks to months but no word from her filtered back. I became frantic as other stories—stories of mass arrest and persecution—were filtering through to fill the pages of the newspapers. I applied for the inevitable visa and documents now necessary to enter and move about in the newly formed "Peoples' Democracies" of Eastern Europe, but, as expected, each application was refused with utter finality.

By early November 1949 I had had enough. I declared my own private war and decided to invade the Peoples' Republic of Socialist Czechoslovakia in my own way. The odds were hopeless from the start. The border was infested with patrols, watch-towers, machine-gun nests and belts of electrified barbed wire. I even had the West Germans to contend with since through purely—and ironically—humanitaian reasons they were inclined to dissuade expeditions such as mine from setting out. However, I chose a dark night for my nefarious purpose and before dawn was eight kilometres inside Czechoslovak territory with most of the obstacles behind me.

"Defence in depth" was a phrase from out of the military training manuals which should have rung bells in my mind as I crossed a railway bridge instead of wading the shallow river near the first township that had not been cleared of its civilian inhabitants. I paid for the indiscretion by finding myself staring down the barrels of six sub-machine carbines. Had it been just one I might have done something about it but six was certain suicide. I went quietly. From the patrol leader I learnt one reason for my success up to that point. The defences faced inwards. Nobody was expected to want to enter the country!

My interrogation lasted two days and they threw the book at me. Spying, smuggling, illegal border crossing, insulting the regime, criminal intent, the lot. At a conservative estimate I made my sentence around sixty years. I served the best part of six weeks of it in the

14

political prison at Cheb. Towards the end of this period I was con-fronted with Dana and in a mockery of a "trial" before a Peoples' Court in Cheb town hall I was officially divested of my spouse. Phrases like "the impossibility of a progressive Czech national being able to live in a decadent bourgeois society" floated down to me but a slice of cake one of my guards was attempting to smuggle me occupied most of my attention. Intense hunger is a great leveller of values.

Back at home my father had learnt of my predicament. He went into action at once and enlisted the aid of Mr. R. A. Butler (later Lord Butler), Member of Parliament for Saffron Walden and resident of Halstead, my home town. The news was flashed to the Foreign Secretary, Ernest Bevin, and from him to Sir Pierson Dixon, our Ambassador in Prague. A full scale diplomatic incident broke out chiefly around the fact that the Czechs had failed to observe the niceties of civilised behaviour. Tiring of the pressure, and possibly fearing for their trade in the Western hemisphere, the Czechs released me one morning before Christmas. The West Germans, not to be robbed of their pound of flesh, promptly arrested me for illegally entering their territory. But I had had enough too and raised such a storm that they let me go next day. Filthy, unshaven, penniless and wifeless I got to Hannover where I threw myself on the mercy of friends.

My divorce under Czech law became valid immediately. British law of course required a three-year period of "suspended animation" to elapse. Thus I was soon to be in the ridiculous position of being married to a woman with another husband and three children! They were sad, empty years only enlivened by one incident that again was to be an integral piece of apparatus in the machinery of my life.

I was in Yorkshire on a foundry sand course when a letter with a Czech postmark arrived. It was from a girl named Vlasta I had met briefly in the school of Dana's home town. She made the startling request that I marry her so that she could legally leave her country and join her fiance now in Australia. She enclosed a photograph of herself. I had no particular "matrimonial intentions" pending at the time and, looking at the shapely features I concluded that the marriage part of the bargain might have its moments! But another divorce? No! I did not care so much about the likely damage to my respect-ability as the monotony of further protracted procedures in British Courts of Law. However, there was no question of either as I was still handicapped by my "period of quarantine" and I thought the incident was closed.

A few months later I learnt that Vlasta had successfully escaped from Czechoslovakia and, by way of East Germany, had landed up at a refugee camp in Munster, Westphalia. Would I go and see her?

I could hardly grudge the girl this small service so for a week we both became inmates of a displaced persons community. For some months we kept in touch. I sent her a few necessities of life and then she moved to Brindisi on the first stage of her journey to Australia. And that was that—or so I thought.

But it still wasn't quite all. Letters, again with Czech postmarks, began arriving at my home. However, they were not for me. Not at first anyway. Vlasta's worried parents, anxious to keep in contact with their daughter, had evolved a scheme in which one of Vlasta's school friends would write letters to me for onward transmission to Australia. I was in fact simply a post-office. I saw no reason not to collaborate especially as my schoolmaster friend had confirmed the scheme's integrity.

Occasionally a letter to me was inserted and I learnt that my "opposite number" in this postal chain was a girl called Jarka Anna. She sounded nice and I encouraged the new fragile friendship. I was suspicious and confused, too, perhaps not without reason. Eventually, a quicker method involving direct postal contact with Australia dissolved the reasons for Jarka Anna maintaining communications with England. To my delight however her letters to me did not cease.

We soon found that we had everything in common. We liked and disliked the same things, thought similar thoughts and our aspirations ascended a parallel path. Her photographs, too, showed a very beautiful girl. But my suspicions still refused to abate. At the back of my mind lurked an idea that this was a much deeper game on the Vlasta theme and, with the three year period over, my defences were down. With a will I got involved in friendships with other girls, French, German, Swiss, Finnish. Even English. Through them all the vision of Jarka Anna persisted.

Then came an edict from the Czech regime forbidding marriage with foreign nationals. It swept away my lingering doubts for the letters still came and the deep feelings we felt for each other continued to be expressed in both directions. But more practical problems arose as we surveyed the obstacles in our path.

I had still to see her and she me, however, before I would commit my life to this trusting girl and, in my book, this meant just that.

For her to come to me was out of the question. For me to go to her would require a miracle.

So it would have to be the miracle.

Even at this point the question "How did you meet your wife?" is only partly answered. Perhaps by this time the polite questioner is sufficiently intrigued to ask a variation of the same query. "How did you make Jarka Anna your wife?"

To answer it means yet another story.

CHAPTER 1

Formidable Appointment

The Channel crossing had not proved an optimistic omen for the future and, green of face, I leaned drunkenly against the ship's rail watching with rabbit-like fascination the frothing waves hurling themselves against the hull. My expensive lunch, taken on this Belgian boat, lay many fathoms deep, but the only desire in my mind was to experience the wonderful immobility of Ostend harbour.

A fellow-passenger with whom I had spoken a few words over the too-rich pork and cabbage lunch came up to me full of confidence and vigour.

"Come and have a beer, old boy," he said. "It'll do the old tummy good."

Through half-closed lids I surveyed my well-meaning tormentor and wondered why it was that some people could remain so disgustingly healthy on these choppy crossings while others, like me, had to suffer. It wasn't as if it was a new experience either, for over the years I had been going backwards and forwards like a yo-yo. My look of uncomprehending misery must have been misinterpreted for the acquaintance died as abruptly as it had blossomed.

Even when the crane jibs hovered over the deck Ostend harbour was a million miles away. Futile voices raised in panic assailed my ears as I was caught up in the shuffling migration towards where somebody thought the gangplank might be. It was, of course, as I at last sidled up to it the exit for those holding red landing tickets. I held a blue one and was acidly directed elsewhere. Another migration carried me relentlessly to another hold in the iron prison and the firm concrete of the dock loomed nearer.

As if to make amends for the shortcomings of the shipping line, the tall-hatted Belgian customs inspectors waved through the surging Easter influx without so much as a glance, and a corner of the Rhinegold Express became for me a haven.

To switch my mind from the mutterings of an outraged stomach and in drowsy accompaniment to the beat of the carriage wheels I ruminated anew on the task that lay ahead. Within twenty hours I should perhaps, if all went well, be asking Jarka Anna to become my wife. The destination for our tryst was an old haunt of mine. Hardly one to recommend for so romantic an undertaking, but the forbidden territory of the tense, hostile Czechoslovak-Bavarian border had certain possible conveniences. Even if we got as far as this step it would, I knew, be but the first of a long, maybe hopeless, struggle. The political scene had gone from bad to worse and the Stalinist grip on eastern Europe was at its tightest. In 1953 no freedom whatsoever existed in these enslaved countries and their borders with the West were unnegotiable.

Ruefully I enumerated the factors against the fulfilment of our quest; a totalitarian state allowing nobody to leave its territory, requiring its subjects to marry only among themselves, refusing entry to all foreigners save those actively sympathetic to its cause. Here I smiled grimly to myself remembering the term of imprisonment I had served in one of its political prisons. I could chalk up a handicap to start with and Communist police do not forgive or forget—as I had reason to know from a fresh trail of visa rejections. But I was in love and the world was my oyster. And all the world loves a lover...

In the material sense the journey was similar to others I had made along this same line. The unfinished underground rail system of Brussels was a little less unfinished perhaps and the twin gothic spires of Cologne cathedral rose from a jungle of new buildings instead of the ruins of the old. The neon-lit city of Frankfurt breathed a new prosperity and I envied the sleeping Frankfurters their comfortable beds.

At ancient Wuerzburg, still licking wounds from a not so ancient war, the first grey light of a watery dawn illuminated the haze over the chimney pots as I stretched my legs on the station platform. Coffee being unobtainable I had to content myself with a bottle of beer. A fine Bavarian lager, but at four in the morning on an empty stomach, no...

The Rhinegold Express and I parted company at Nuremberg. The timetable still demanded five hours of heel-kicking until the once-daily Orient Express from Paris put in an appearance.

I was not unacquainted with this fascinating Bavarian city and, before leaving the busy station, made straight for the mens' washrooms where ten pfennigs procured a most worthwhile wash and shave. A further outlay produced a period of privacy in the toilet, though the ration of both paper and privacy was severely limited. This I had learnt from earlier experience and the invading presence of the large and totally unabashed woman attendant. Now, however, my foot was planted firmly against the door.

Breakfast in a comfortable *gasthaus* dominated by the battlements of the patched-up castle consisted of a series of omelettes each washed down by handleless cups of coffee. The fact that it was not yet seven o'clock made not the slightest difference to the friendly and efficient service. My stomach proclaimed its contentment.

Considerably refreshed, I strolled into the castle grounds and, as the morning sun dispelled the clinging remnants of dawn mist, found myself a seat overlooking the sprawling city. From innumerable chimney pots their plumes of smoke rose perpendicularly into the thin air as innumerable families brewed their breakfast coffee. Directly below, men and women were noisily erecting their colourful market stalls, but their shouted pleasantries were already drowned in the sullen rumble as Nuremberg awoke to another day in her chequered history.

In spite of its past associations I felt an urge to linger in the safe solid streets amongst the hospitable citizens. The border with the other world was no more than fifty miles away and even here made its evil presence felt. I kicked myself for being a fool. After all, I was attempting nothing lethal this trip. To do so would have been plain stupidity. Even a cat would set off the mines. No, I was simply going to remain on the Orient Express as it made the lonely journey across the long frontier.

There would be complications, of course. Would the West German border people let me through upon learning I had no Czech entry permits? And what about the Czech authorities? Of course there would be a passport inspection, but would it occur before the border town of Cheb was reached? The meeting with Jarka Anna depended upon this, and my being able to see her before or while they were finding out I had no visa. And Jarka Anna herself? Even if the telegram I had sent her from England had reached her would she be able to act upon my request to be at Cheb railway station at three o'clock this very afternoon?

Her small figure of the photographs rose to fill my imagination and again the trust and devotion she carried for me touched my heart. Had my telegram been thoughtless and put her into any kind of danger? Cheb was ten kilometres inside Czechoslovakia and outside the border zone. But it was still a restricted area and would require a permit. I had told myself that no possible harm could arise from asking a girl to meet me in her own country. But I was fast learning the ways of Communism ...

The Orient Express hissed into the station half an hour before schedule, but I was there to meet it. Few people remained in the great express and not only did I have empty compartments to choose from but also whole empty carriages. The absence of fellow-passengers was accentuated by the number of discarded newspapers, magazines and fruit peelings scattered about. Even the seats were warm.

From Nuremberg onwards the train stopped at every station as if to display a reluctance to leave this last sanctuary of Western Germany. The multiple greens of the wooded country-side, intersected with clear tinkling streams and rocky hillocks, increased in profusion while the April sun bathed every new scene in glowing warmth. Each village, huddled at the foot of its onion-domed church, came straight out of a fairy-tale.

I could generate little in the way of an appetite, but made it my duty to down an ample *wurst* sandwich and a bottle of beer. After all, food was not likely to figure very largely in the events of the next few hours. I had just time to accomplish the chore when the train drew into the German border village of Schirnding.

The station had not changed one iota since my last visit. It was as if I was seeing a film performance round for the second time. There was the little group of green *Grenzpolizei* waiting to board the train, looking efficient and smug as do all Germans in uniform. And the *Bundesbahn* signalman, dressed as an admiral of the fleet, scowling at the train from his little office window with the cares of the whole state transport system on his shoulders. I looked at my watch and noticed we were exactly on time.

"Guten tag, mein Herr," said a voice behind me. I turned and smiled back at the piano keyboard of gold teeth into which I was looking.

"You stay on the train?", he went on with an air of incredulity as he perceived that I was making no effort to leave the train.

I nodded. The usual vague feeling of annoyance passed over me as I realised that he had correctly typed me as British. I could read his mind. 'Here is an idiot. Therefore he must be British. Q.E.D'.

"Passport, bitte," he snapped out suddenly mindful of his business.

Slowly he flicked through the pages, gazing solicitously at the jungle of rubber stamps. Twice he went through the book; then gave up. He looked at me and the gold teeth slid from view.

"To where are you going?"

"Prag," I replied, optimistically.

"Have you a tschechisch visa?"

"No, do I need one?" I made it sound as I had never heard of technicalities like visas.

"Then you must leave the train hier, mein Herr; things nicht gut da." The policeman dazzled me with a smile again and indicated the direction of the Czech frontier.

Without further ado I collected my one travelling bag from the rack and made as if to depart. The German, obviously convinced now that the British were complete fools, saluted and proceeded on his way along the corridor.

After a glance around, with bag in hand I slipped unobtrusively into the toilet at the end of the carriage and there remained while the train performed a series of shunting operations. Through a patch of clear glass in the frosted window I watched the Czech locomotive, an impressive mass of smoke stacks and piston rods with a large red star emblazoned on the front of the massive boiler, clank disdainfully by to take over from its lesser German rival.

A knock at the door produced a moment of consternation, but it was only the Customs wanting to know if I was taking any coffee out of the country.

"No," I said, and manufactured some sound effects in tune with my immediate surroundings to discourage further discourse.

A few minutes later there was a movement, more than a shunt, and, chalking up round one to me, I emerged from hiding. Back in my compartment I watched the passing countryside with ominous fascination. Not only was it my happy hunting ground of a few years back, but through those empty fields ran the most deadly frontier in the world.

The great Orient Express, reduced now to a three-coach local, crawled at a walking pace along the single line that formed the only rail link connecting the two countries. It was difficult to say when the territory became Czech, though I knew that a line of posts existed to offer the information to mad dogs and Englishmen who braved the no-mans land to read them. I studied each railway crossing cabin and lane but saw no sign of habitation or movement. We were in a vacuum that was neither East nor West.

I jumped out of my skin as the door of my compartment slid open. It was the Czech ticket inspector wanting to see my ticket which, since it was made out to Cheb, produced no comment. We smiled at each other and I almost had myself believing that he felt the urge for human companionship too.

Outside the woods grew thicker. I tried to pick out the landmarks of my previous ill-fated night operation* again and failed. Nothing moved; not a grazing cow, a spring lamb, a bird. Even the breeze held its breath.

Suddenly the new frontier was before my eyes. A ploughed strip of land—appropriately named the zone of death—ran like a poisonous viper through wood, village and field killing all that lay athwart its path. It snaked its way through a desolation of jagged stumps, all that remained after the trees had been dynamited and the wood destroyed. The ruins of a complete village—a village that had even been divested of its name—and a farmhouse, empty and decaying, marked its course. Beside the innocuous-looking furrow ran a double wall of barbed wire with insulators, like obscene white growths, amongst the rusted barbs. At intervals timber watchtowers brooded over the whole satanic apparatus.

The train drew to a chastened halt a moment later and I saw we had reached a wayside halt just out of sight of the wire fence. At least I was once again in the land that held my destiny though how long I would remain upon its sacred soil was questionable.

*November 1949 (see page 14)

CHAPTER 2

Border Engagement

Only the ghosts of passengers boarded or alighted from the depleted Orient Express at the wayside halt. Even the train itself had become an ethereal thing, a shadow of its former glory with only the destination boards defiantly proclaiming the exotic cities of Europe.

But if fare-paying passengers failed to throng its plush interior, others did. Encumbered by an arsenal of weapons half a battalion from the security forces of the new order took over the train. From the window I watched squads of khaki-clad soldiery invade the corridors while others, in overalls, proceeded to investigate the bogies and mechanism beneath the coaches in an apparent search for stowaways. The remainder took up strategic positions at the four corners of the train to await the expected flushing out of Western agents.

My solitude was rudely shattered. A soldier of the frontier force bearing a submachine gun and two days growth of beard swung open the door of my compartment. He stopped short at the sight of me and a look of startled surprise spread across his lean stubbly face.

I said "Guten tag" because my Czech wasn't good enough, but he made no reply. The sight of a real passenger had been too much for him.

Recovering, he resumed his duties peering under the seats and up at the luggage racks. Another man joined him giving me a long hard look and almost decapitating himself with the bayonet of his rifle as he and his accoutrements stuck in the doorway. So far everybody was much too busy to ask for my passport.

Left severely alone I kept away from the window in case an officer or someone in authority took it into his head to inspect the papers of the freak in the second coach. But nothing happened and there was a glow of triumph in my heart as the train moved forward with an angry jerk. I noticed several guards had transferred themselves to the outside steps of my coach and were riding with the train. But they were of no consequence to me. Feverishly I chalked up round two.

It really did seem as if I was going to make it. The next stop must be Cheb for the train's scheduled arrival there was well overdue. Picking up speed, the Orient Express attempted to regain a little of its lost reputation though its timetable was sadly awry when the first houses of the town hove into view. Rattling and clacketting over the points we began to slow down. Full of excitement, my heart beating like a tom-tom, I leaned far out of the window, ignoring the showers of smuts, craning my neck to catch the first glimpse of the girl who had drawn me to these inhospitable parts.

Beneath a footbridge bearing a red star and the word "peace" in five languages, I saw her. She was standing alone, a solitary figure on a nearly empty platform. Before the train stopped our eyes met.

I experienced a tangle of emotions. Triumph, joy, pride eagerness and a surge of tenderness all tore at my heart. I watched Jarka Anna walk towards my coach.

The train stopped. I awaited the expected invasion of customs, immigration and general law and order. But nothing happened. A moment of perplexity and then it hit me. They weren't expecting any passengers! In a flash I was in the corridor and off the train.

Five seconds later Jarka Anna was in my arms. I kissed her hard on the mouth and caught a whiff of fragrant scent. I closed my eyes and recorded the moment for eternity.

Breathlessly I broke the silence. "Did you have any trouble getting here?" I asked anxiously. I gazed into the turquoise blue eyes for the first time in my life.

"No, but did you?" The reply was in a firm voice without a trace of hesitation at the unfamiliar tongue.

"Not yet, anyway," I said glancing ominously towards my recently vacated coach in which sounds of movement indicated that somebody had learnt of the existence of a passenger.

"But listen darling, in a minute those wolves will be on to us but there's something I want to give you first."

While I fumbled in my pocket my eyes took in the girl before me. It was as if her photograph had come alive. The dark hair cascaded on to her shoulders framing a face that held both joy and sadness. She was smaller than I had expected but her slim body was lithe and beautiful. I looked at the dark lines beneath her eyes and I knew the reason. I knew too that Jarka Anna was for me.

"There's no time for pretty words, but you understand I love you and want you to be my wife and—well, I've brought our engagement ring." The rush of words spilt over the girl as my eyes tried to hold her own and watch for the approach of authority at the same time. Then, ignoring the threat, I looked her straight in the face and added, "you will marry me, won't you?"

The smile upon Jarka Anna's lips grew tender and her eyes were moist. She held up the third finger of her left hand and nodded her head, unable to trust herself to speak.

I flung myself into her arms again and kissed her long and forcibly. The second time we came up for air more practical moves seemed desirable. Still no interruption came from the authorities. All we had to do was to walk out of the station and damn the consequences. Gently I led my fiancee towards the exit.

We had only taken a dozen steps when the shout came at us. We stopped to meet the onslaught of outraged officialdom.

"Here comes trouble," I whispered resignedly and felt the squeeze of her hand.

A security police officer stormed up to us and a flood of indignant Czech surged around our ears. He got as good as he gave however for Jarka Anna, her chin tilted, responded with similar gusto. Uncomprehending I waded in.

"If anyone's got to be blamed for anything it'd better be me."

The man quietened down upon hearing English. Still ruffled however he wanted to know why I had left the train.

"Because nobody said otherwise," I replied pleased to note that he could speak a little of my language.

"And who gave you permission to speak to this girl?"

Indignation boiled within me. I stifled a rude retort.

"Why shouldn't I speak to my fiancee?" I demanded instead.

"How long have you been engaged?"

"About four minutes," I said.

"Your passport please." The officer, obviously at a loss for words, took refuge in the little blue book. I didn't think he would be at a loss for long when he found I had no visa. Like his German predecessor he thumbed through the pages and twice came back to an out-of-date Czech visa stamp of ancient vintage.

"This visa is out of date," he proclaimed loudly.

"Yes," I said.

The policeman stared at me for a moment, a bewildered expression crossing his face. I began to feel sorry for him. Behind the swarthy mildly handsome features I detected a man with a heart.

"Come with me, both of you. You will have to return immediately, Mr. — er — Portway. And no talking." The staccato instructions

26

poured out of him. He retained my passport.

Crossing the tracks we were escorted to his office in the administrative section of the station buildings. A number of other policemen were lounging about the poky little room and rancid tobacco smoke rose in clouds to the ceiling.

Our entry aroused considerable interest. Ignoring the respectful questions of his subordinates the officer sat down behind a desk and from his little edifice of power commenced to pump Jarka Anna for information.

There followed a long telephone call to S.N.B.* headquarters in Prague. He had to repeat his piece to three different departments, the last requiring it yet again at dictation speed, before he could receive and acknowledge instructions. Relieved of some of his responsibility the man became less taciturn.

"Sorry," he said to me, "but your girl, she goes home." Escorted by a colleague Jarka Anna was removed from the room.

"May I—," I began.

"I must get your statement on to paper," broke in the officer hastily as if anticipating my request.

"But I haven't made a statement."

"Your girl has."

It seemed to be adequate.

The officer's typing was about half as good as my own. And I'm a one-finger man. With great intensity he thumped out the details on an old Remington, banging wrong keys and forgetting words in mid-sentence. Four carbon copies of the statement had to be completed since it appeared that our particular "crime" fitted none of the forms provided.

"You **did** say you came to become engaged to be married?" he asked, frowning at his handiwork.

I said that was the general idea.

A few more thumps and back-spacing and the job was done. The man signed the top copy with a flourish. I thought that if nothing else it was an extremely dogged performance.

I stood up. "Now may I go and see her again please?"

"No." The refusal came abrupt and final.

I looked at him and my eyes were hard.

*Straz Narodni Bezpecnosti (The Security Police)

27

"She is my future wife and I've come all this way to see her. Let me at least say goodbye."

"My orders are that you are not to have further contact with her," replied the officer, but he didn't look at me. Nor did he seem to know about my previous and more serious "crime" of illegal border crossing. Perhaps I should have been thankful for small mercies.

My voice was a rasp. "This country must be getting pretty low if a man is refused permission to say goodbye to his fiancee". I noticed that some of the other policemen were listening.

The officer was weakening. "It's against orders," he repeated defensively.

I tried a new approach. "When does she leave?" I asked.

"On the next train to Prague." He glanced at the clock on the wall. "It goes in ten minutes."

"Come with me ," I said and led the officer out of the door.

"You can see her for just one minute" he acquiesced, catching me up in an attempt to show who was escorting whom.

The Orient Express was still waiting. It had been moved to No. 1 platform and was "dressed up" again in the garb of a transcontinental express. Eight more coaches, including the blue and gold wagon-lit sleepers, and a restaurant car had been added and, with its blue-uniformed staff fussing round it, gave no indication of the degradation to which it had been subjected.

Ignoring my companion I walked briskly along the length of the train staring in at the windows. The coaches were full now and there was even an overflow in the corridors.

She was in the fifth coach. A frontier guard stood ostentatiously outside her window. Ignoring him too I rapped on the window. Swiftly Jarka Anna left her seat to emerge on to the platform smiling happily.

"I've come to say goodbye, but on stolen time," I explained softly.

The smile faded slightly. "A long way to come for so short a time together," she said. Again the infinite sadness was in her voice.

"I'd come again tomorrow if I'd do any good." And then the dam burst. All the sweet nothings that are everything to a girl and a boy in love came out. All the plans, hopes and intentions that we knew in our hearts could never be were shared between us. And all around the people in the corridor, who had learnt of an Englishman in their midst, crowded round in friendly encouragement nodding and smiling as if they too were a part of our lives.

Stolidly ignoring everyone Jarka Anna and I spoke our few last words together.

"You'll wait for me Jarka Anna darling?", I said in a broken voice.

She saw my misery and quickly changed the subject. "Call me Anna," she whispered, "it's easier for English people. After all I will be one, too, soon. . ." She had answered my question.

A whistle blew. To the delight of the audience I took Anna into my arms and kissed her passionately. The officer coughed and tapped me on the shoulder. The guard shuffled his feet. A low growl, an embryo snarl of anger, swept through the crowd. For the first time I became aware of the mood of the people around me and their interest and sympathy in the little drama unfolding before them. They seemed to know what was happening.

The whistle was for another train, but the time of departure for the express was due. Anna suddenly buried her face in my shoulder to hide her tears. I felt the trembling of her body and a sickness in my throat. Stroking her hair I murmured, "Soon I'll come back, darling, whatever they do."

Her voice, muffled by my jacket, was almost inaudible.

"Yes, dearest one, come back. Please come back."

Another whistle shrilled. There came the banging of doors. Swiftly Anna slipped back into the train. In a mixture of tongues the crowd assailed me with questions and advice. I looked into the sea of kind simple faces and tried to grin my gratitude for their support.

The train slid forward. For a moment I saw the slim figure at the window. I turned to my escort. "Thanks," I said, "thank you very much."

For the next hour or two the bottom fell out of my world. I learnt that I was to be deported on the next westbound train which did not leave until the early hours of the next day. I suppose I should have felt grateful but in my depressed state the news only served to increase my misery. I was to be sent away from Anna and that seemed the worst punishment of all. With my fiancee departed and my passport confiscated, authority relaxed its grip. Many a wild scheme was hatched and rejected as I watched the evening light dapple the roofs of the town that had twice formed a backcloth to my destiny.

Diversion came from an unexpected quarter. A group of off-duty border guards swung into the station and made for the bar. Someone must have told them about me for a moment later I was invited to join them. Thus for an hour I swigged down tankards of sweet brown beer and attempted conversation with a group of thugs who, I was pleased to note, were not entirely inhuman.

In a mixture of languages the complicated conversation ranged from politics to popsies. With an eye to the main chance I enquired idly about their jobs. What were the duties of a border guard? Were there any gaps in the fence? How were the mines placed? What happened to anyone caught trying to escape? What action was taken to stop anyone trying to come in?

This last question was met with a bellow of laughter and a variety of replies which, boiled down, could be transcribed as "send him to a lunatic asylum!" But my veiled interrogation produced no vital gems of knowledge, no glaring loophole in a chain that fettered a nation.

In a considerably more cheerful mood I was halfway through a demonstration of British arms drill with the aid of a borrowed carbine when the officer appeared at the door. He showed signs of acute displeasure. The weapon was snatched from my hand and both demonstration and party ended abruptly. My new friends became once more the faceless ones of the state security machine.

Half an hour after midnight I was escorted to my seat in another section of the Orient Express. It was destined for the Munich route which, for me, would mean spending the remainder of the night in some desolate West German railway station. The officer gave me a short speech of farewell and an icy recitation on the subject of valid visas. He saluted and withdrew. But outside my carriage door the policeman remained.

At the border the same rigmarole took place. It took longer presumably because there was better reason for the search. In a shower of sparks the train rattled into Schirnding. A familiar figure appeared at the door and the gold teeth blazed in a gigantic smile.

"Guten abend, mein Herr," it said, "we hoped you'd be coming back on this train."

CHAPTER 3

Yugoslav Interlude

The swarthy official jabbed the blank space on the form and shouted "Yes, please". Though the two words were his full vocabulary of English I knew quite well what he meant. I had watched two Frenchmen get the same treatment a few minutes before. It appeared imperative that the authorities learn the travellers' immediate destination. It was a matter of grave importance, of state security, of life and death. I nodded knowingly, glanced at the map on the Customs House wall and entered "Ljubljana". Quite content, Mr. "Yes, please" took my form, repeated his vocabulary and saw me off on the road— to Rijeka.

This was Yugoslavia in 1953. A land struggling silently to rid itself of Soviet domination. The trappings of militant Communism remained but in the summer of that year this one Iron Curtain country opened its gates to the first hesitant tourists from a not so despised West. I was premature but I thought I saw the writing on the wall.

At any rate, I packed a bag and, with a little eight-horsepower Wolseley, set out to see how things ticked. Since Yugoslavia possessed no common border with Czechoslovakia I expected no great revelations, but my homeward itinerary would bring me close to the Austro-Czech frontier and the scene of a proposed second tryst with my fiancee.

Far away to the north Anna waited. Her application to marry me delivered at the cold impersonal offices of the Czech Ministry of the Interior in Prague, there was nothing else to do but wait. She left her job as a secretary and translator in a state import-export agency so that, unemployed, she would be a more likely candidate for her own exportation. Instead all there was left was a drab lonely life at home. Most of my letters reached her safely and now she began to receive almost daily picture postcards of exciting places long denied her and her fellow-countrymen. One of these was postmarked Zagreb and that for me was when the trouble started. But that's later.

At a point somewhere north of Crkvenica the road southwards, marked on the map as a bold red line, had been transformed into little more than a pot-holed cart-track. True, a notice thoughtfully printed in English, in addition to Serbo-Croat, indicated that a poor surface could be expected on the next stretch of highway, but this

31

gave little clue to the unwary motorist that these conditions prevailed for nearly a thousand kilometres right down to the Albanian border, and even further if one was taking the coast road to Greece. I later learnt of a similar notice of typical Yugoslav inadequacy which faced in the opposite direction, on the last fifty kilometres of metalled road leading in from the Grecian frontier.

Dallying where I could in the towns and villages I met on the road south was fun. Englishmen and English cars were a rarity and both produced large friendly crowds at every halt. Once I unwisely left the car unlocked for a moment as I dived into a shop for provisions. Upon my return I found three local inhabitants squeezed into the front excitedly pressing knobs and waiting for something to ·happen. The usual two dozen onlookers crowded round offering encouragement.

Accommodation, even of the three star variety, was ridiculously cheap. The State Tourist Agency just hadn't a clue as to standard Western hotel charges, though regrettably they were soon to learn. The August sun was a ball of fire and the greater part of my sojourns were spent immersed in the Adriatic which was the only sensible place to be in temperatures that rarely fell below ninety degrees. Rijeka, which was to figure in another small drama in my life at a later date, the resort of Crkvenica, Senj, a small township clinging tenaciously to the side of a grey boulder infested hillside. Each I classified by their ease of access to deep water and the speed with which I could immerse my hot and sticky body.

At a steady 15 m.p.h., which was as fast as the car could proceed without disintegration on the broken road surface, I turned inland near Senj. In a series of exaggerated alpine bends the road snaked up the low hills giving, if you allowed the permanent cloud of dust to settle, a fine view of a vivid blue arm of sea forcing its way into the barren land surrounding the bay.

The dust was my closest companion. The evil-smelling Yugoslav petrol necessitated all car windows to be open so that my half-naked sweat-streaked body was grey with the stuff. Occasionally the road played a game. A sudden improvement, a brief inspired section of tarmac and the car, unleashed, would race forward to fall with a series of rending crashes into a hidden tank trap round the next corner. In addition to the dust and the road were the antics of my fellow travellers. A peasant lady of ample girth stopped me dead by the simple expedient of standing in the middle of the road. She wanted a lift to the next village and spent it happily being car-sick all the way there. Policemen, draped in the usual assortment of lethal iron-mongery, sprang out on me bristling with officialdom, only to demand a preview of my symbol of Western luxury, the car (one of them did remember to look at my passport but held it upside-down!). Herds of cows escorted by grinning Yugoslav cowboys who found it a huge joke to have me accompany them, swearing and hooting, for mile after plodding mile.

At Gospic I ran out of petrol. This is fatal in Yugoslavia, or it was then. I was depending upon Gospic for my map informed me that it was an important enough town to possess a petrol pump. But my map had not kept up with events for the pump had been out of use since the war. In front of me lay the arid Velebit Mountains and I had no wish for my skeleton to lie bleaching there. "Go to the railway station," they said. The railway station, it seemed, had taken over from the church as the fountainhead of wisdom and knowledge. So emptying my last can of juice into the thirsty car I made tracks for the station.

A pantomime scene enacted in the office of the station-master eventually clarified my requirements and, beaming all over his face, that worthy produced the solution to the problem. In two hours the Istanbul-Trieste "Benzine Special" was due. He, Marko Rankovic, would stop the great express, he, Marco, would do anything for an Englishman, and in the meantime come, a little refreshment. The train was, of course, late which was unfortunate since we were both suffering from a surfeit of slivovice when the long line of tanker wagons drew in to the accompaniment of indignant whistles from the powerful locomotive objecting to the upraised signal arm.

In a daze I drew the car up against one of the wagons where we flooded everything, including the tank and my spare cans, in a deluge of petrol. The locomotive driver and his fireman then had to be mollified with a further distribution of slivovice, a period of time which at least allowed the sea of petrol, in which my car stood like an island, to evaporate safely. Vaguely I enquired about payment. My new friends laughed heartily. The very idea. The petrol didn't belong to them. Contemptibly they indicated southwards. The Italians wouldn't miss it anyway.

I made even less progress than usual that day. Outside Gospic I chose a sheltered spot and slept off the excesses of my petrol delivery. The map promised a certain amount of scenic grandeur and the road a lot more dust.

Both promises were amply fulfilled. Through gaps in the billowing yellow cloud appeared a country of strange lunar rock formations twisted into ethereal shapes of savage beauty. Wild, cruel, pitiless country that sent the first trickle of loneliness into my heart.

The descent to Zadar took many hours and a blood-red sunset, reflecting its glory in the smooth sea, welcomed me to the ancient city of cherries. In spite of a film of oil and a sprinkling of dead fish in the port I managed to emerge from the water cleaner than I went in.

It was a spur-of-the-moment decision that caused me to garage the car in the town and take to a life afloat. The daily steamship service between Zadar and Dubrovnik suddenly became a most attractive mode of travel with no dust, petrol, fumes or pot-holes.

Certain alternative disadvantages became apparent, however, as the voyage got under way. The old tub boasted no capitalist luxuries like cabins or bunks. Instead one staked a claim on the deck and held it against all comers. Not in the know, I was ruefully contemplating the prospect of a night on my feet when I spied a vacant space before a closed door. Gingerly stepping over the carpet of prostrate humanity I descended upon my prize and lay down on the hard boards. A short while later I learnt why the space was vacant when the door flew open to make violent contact with my head and a large foot descended upon my stomach. Half stunned and gasping for breath I was treated to a tirade on nautical procedure by the chief engineer before he realised that the battered patron was an Englishman. Instantly the smile, the apologies and the solution to the problem appeared like magic; the solution being the forcible closing up of a line of grunting bodies so that there was room for me out of harm's way.

Sibenik, Split and a shoal of fairy-tale islands provided gay diversion the next day. At Split there was time for a stroll in the pine-bordered streets. My return to the ship coincided with the embarkation of a battalion of Young Pioneers. With frying-pans, tin mugs and daggers swinging like flails these "Boy Scouts" hurled themselves frenziedly up the narrow gang plank, sweeping aside the knot of harbour officials and two tommy-gun toting militiamen. Somewhat awed I followed across the wreckage.

Dubrovnik was a shock until I realised that its port was quite a separate entity. The hotch-potch of factories and warehouses hardly reconciled themselves to what I had heard of the fabulous city of Emperor Maximilian. But an ancient tram— probably a legacy of the Emperor himself—rattled me across the narrow peninsula to the city centre.

In spite of the historic charm, worn like a cloak by Dubrovnik's city walls and cloistered streets, my return to civilisation was the terminus for those brief few days of happy freedom from the cares of life. I had been alone but happy and every stranger was my friend. Now I became just another guest in a luxury hotel—the Argentina—and though amongst fellow foreigners I was desperately alone.

The swimming was idyllic, the hotel service fit for a king, but these by themselves are no recipe for happiness. Though I pretended otherwise I was simply marking time. The nightly ritual of an exquisite dinner on a bougainvillea-splashed terrace overlooking the twinkling lights of the town and the dark hump of the island of Lok became, for me, an ordeal.

My eyes wandered over to the other diners. Young couples mostly, with here and there a family group. Alone, conspicuously silent, I caught snatches of light-hearted conversation and gusts of laughter while the ready-laid cutlery opposite me mocked my solitude.

On the fifth evening, with my last plum brandy, I toasted my resolve to see again within ten days this girl who could torment me so. I left next morning and the open road became my elixir simply because it led to her.

CHAPTER 4

Ambush in Austria

From the Argentina Hotel in Dubrovnik to doss-house was quite a jolt. But at one in the morning no other establishment sent an emissary to the harbour to meet the boat from Dubrovnik. So the doss-house it was.

A blowsy old crone met me on the quay and made me signs, one of which was the international gesture for sleep. Whether one was supposed to sleep with her, her daughter or if a selection existed was not clear, but I was agreeably relieved to be taken by rowing boat to a tumbledown house containing a dormitory for down and outs with no other commitment involved.

I awoke considerably refreshed, reasonably unbitten and still in possession of my wallet. Washing apparently was not included in the tariff so, after paying a grossly inflated charge, which brought the establishment's rating somewhere on a par with the Argentina, I left to locate the car.

It was Sunday and the hour was early. But that made no difference. Not only was the car ready but so was the garage proprietor's breakfast in which I was invited to participate. The whole family saw me off as I headed once more into my cloud of dust.

Two days later I was in Zagreb. A large modern city, it had little to hold me. I was now car camping so I purchased some groceries in a flourishing private enterprise market before investigating the cathedral and sending a postcard to Anna saying "wish you were here"— and meaning it. I also added that I hoped to see her on the Czech border a week hence. In a shower of rain, which at least laid the dust, I headed north.

The route to Maribor, if you go by way of Varazdin and Pluj, could, even then, be described as a road. Between the potholes occasional traces of tarmac were discernable. To make up for an absence of meandering cows the Yugoslav Army obliged with large quantities of horse-drawn artillery. They too took little notice of my incessant hooting but were considerably less charming about it.

At the Austrio-Yugoslav frontier a few miles north of Maribor I was interrogated on my financial status.

"How much Yugoslav money have you?" they asked.

"Two thousand dinars," I replied, remembering a rule concerning a restriction imposed upon the amount of dinars allowed out of the country. I also remembered an additional 5,000-dinar note that reposed in my wallet.

"Only one thousand dinars is allowed out of the People's Federated Republic," barked the official, who was a better linguist than Mr. "Yes, please". "Goods to the value of your remaining dinars may be obtained at the kiosk."

Thus I bade farewell, not without reluctance, to Yugoslavia and, with a car weighed down with the control post's entire stock of home-made cheese, I entered the fair territory of Austria. The customs examination their side of the border was non-existent—possibly thanks to the cheese, which was not without its Yugoslav characteristics.

The Austrian road surface was a treat and for the first time for many days the speedometer needle passed the 30 m.p.h. mark. I watched the phenomenon with delight and saw it climb higher and higher as the car sped like a released bird through the hilly countryside. At Graz I stopped to exchange my 5,000 dinars and buy a map. The bank official eyed my note with distaste, finally offering me a few schillings. Rarely has a map cost me the equivalent of £2.10. 0.

At the approaches to the Semmering Pass I left the road and pitched camp in a recently harvested cornfield. It was only late afternoon and I could have made Vienna by nightfall. There was then, however, an inconvenient situation in Austria brought about by the four-power occupation of the country. Except for token forces the western powers had long since removed their troops and restrictions but the Soviet, being the Soviet, still held the eastern half of the country in its grip. Vienna, like Berlin, was an international island set in a Soviet sea and there were but two permitted routes to it from western Austria. I held the necessary "grey card" and other documents in support of my rights to use the Graz route but my nose smelt trouble. And in case my nose was right I would at least face it fresh from a good night's sleep. The Russian zonal border lay just down the road.

I cooked myself a meal of which Yugoslav cheese formed a substantial basis—and when I awoke in the morning trouble had come to me, though not the sort I was expecting. The wheels of my car had sunk deep into the soft earth and though I risked the wrath of the farmer by using his precious corn stooks as anti-skid mats I was well and truly stuck. Eventually I managed to recruit half a dozen harvesters from various points on the landscape and their brawny arms made short work of the situation. I felt mean paying them in the only currency I could afford; Yugoslav cheese!

At the zonal border a British corporal delivered a solemn warning of unknown hazards ahead. His Russian counterpart a hundred yards further on completely disillusioned me with a grin, a salute and by waving me straight through. Except for occasional military lorries, signposts bearing place-names in both German and Russian script and the usual profusion of Communist slogans there was little sign of the occupation. At Wiener Neustadt I took a wrong turning and went ten kilometres off course, but no car-loads of M.G.B.* men came in hot pursuit. My feeling as I drove into Vienna, could almost be described as one of disappointment.

I saw much of the Austrian capital that day. Before leaving England I had been given the name, but not the address, of a Viennese business-man. I traced him through the good offices of the bureau of missing persons but not before learning the hard way that there were two Auhofstrasse's, both at opposite ends of the city.

Herr Zenk and his charming wife entertained me to dinner at a luxurious roof-top restaurant offering, in addition to an excellent meal, a magnificent view of Vienna by night. Far to the east could be seen the glow of the Soviet-worked oil wells that many Austrians believed to be the reason for prolonged Soviet occupation. During the meal I gently prodded my hosts for information about conditions in the Russian zone particularly near the Czech border and it was from this source of information that I formulated my plan.

That night from the room of my hotel in the Kietzing district I composed a letter to Anna. In it I mentioned the date and place of our second tryst; two days hence at the border control point of Horni Dvoriste.

The plan itself was very simple. With Linz, in northern Austria, as a base I would set out by train and alight at the frontier village of Summerau, ten kilometres beyond Freistadt. On the other side of the border, if all went well, Anna would also alight from a train at the little Czech border town of Horni Dvoriste fifty-odd kilometres east of Ceske Budejovice. Six kilometres and a border would then separate us, but because the Austrian side was Soviet occupied the Czech frontier fortifications were unlikely to be unduly impregnable. From then on we would work things according to circumstances and effect a meeting with or without the consent of the border authorities.

*Soviet Security Forces

38

In the morning I left Vienna after confirming the salient points of the arrangement by telegram, for I doubted if the letter would reach her in time. With two full days to go there was ample time to reach Linz, settle in and investigate local conditions. Most of the town was in the American zone, but the suburbs north east of the Danube formed a Soviet sector. There was only one snag. Something overlooked in my calculations. My "grey card" was valid for the Vienna-Graz route only.

The other route was Vienna-Linz, a three or four hour drive. To go via Graz would necessitate an extra two hundred kilometres at least; not to mention a couple of hefty mountain ranges. And there just wasn't time. Keeping my fingers tightly crossed I steered the car on to the Linz road.

Sixty kilometres later, in the outskirts of St. Poelten, I slammed on the brakes as, upon rounding a bend, I came upon a line of cars being subjected to a police check. With a dozen cars ahead I reacted swiftly and, pulling round in a fast turn, made to return Viennawards. An interested patrolman, witness to the car's suspicious behaviour, promptly blocked further progress by placing himself and motor-cycle squarely in my path, the raised arm challenging me to commit manslaughter if I dared. Hastily running through my list of excuses I halted.

"A guilty conscience, Englander?" sneered the man.

"Not in the least," I countered in tones of high dudgeon. "I've forgotten something."

"A grey card for instance?" he suggested. In a more friendly tone he added, "but don't worry; it's only driving licences we want this time."

I relaxed, displayed the required document and prepared to rejoin the line of cars. The policeman saluted and offered a final word of advice, "Careful at Enns Bridge," he said.

I knew what he meant. Enns was the zonal border and there weren't just Austrian policemen there.

An hour later I joined the queue of cars at the approaches to the bridge and proceeded slowly towards the two Russian military police N.C.Os. who were stopping one car in three for a papers examination. But my luck held. The axe fell on the car behind me.

The clocks of Linz were striking midday as the little Wolseley nosed into the city's busy streets. I booked into a modest hotel and began unloading my bits and pieces of baggage. And that wa- when I met Norman Shaw.

A loud voice with the friendliest of Sheffield accents materialised from a passing cyclist. "Hello—how are you—I'm Norman Shaw—working in a local garage—enjoying myself immensely—no closing times here—come and have a drink."

Weakly I said "yes" in reference to the last words of the tirade.

Over several glasses of *dunkelbier* and an immense ham roll we talked. Norman proved a veritable mine of information and I took to him immediately. I released to him a little of my intentions and was straightway offered all the help I could manage. He even had to be gently persuaded from accompanying me to Summerau. Instead, he offered to look after the car in case, as he put it, "something happened."

Together we toured the city, calling on the station, Norman's garage and finally the Danube road bridge. Though a part of Linz the suburb of Urfahr, on the far side of the swiftly flowing river, was in another world. Halfway across the bridge the Soviet checkpoint severed the link far more effectively than the wide waters.

Norman was telling me how the Russians made little effort to control entry into their zone.

"Look, nothing ever happens," he pronounced, walking boldly towards the guardpost. A green-uniformed soldier came forward to meet him and Norman executed a smart about-turn and retreated. But in spite of this I noticed that few individuals or vehicles were, in fact, being stopped.

That evening Norman gathered together some of his many Austrian friends and the ensuing party drove away, for a few carefree hours, the gnawing pangs of anxiety that, again, were nibbling at my mind. To plan a border meeting such as I proposed was easy in the comfort and security of a home or hotel, but the inexorable drawing near of its execution produced the inevitable fit of nerves. But in the gay company of the hard-drinking Fritz, the vivacious blonde Hilda and the host of characters whom Norman collected about him like flies to a flypaper it was not difficult to slip the traces of worry. From *bierhaus* to restaurant, from cafe to cabaret we went, and night became morning.

While we were sipping black coffee in a well-patronised 'Expresso' bar and discussing our next port of call I slipped away to collect reserves of cash from my baggage in the hotel. This was no more than half a kilometre away; just over the railway bridge and first turn left. The night was cold and there were no stars in the sky.

I stepped out briskly not wishing to lose the gathering when they moved on to the next haunt of vice. I found the bridge cloaked in darkness except for a solitary street lamp that accentuated the black shadows thrown against the parapet. There were no houses here, only the dim shapes of warehouses and the gaunt skeleton of a steel pylon carrying the electric current for the railway. Somewhere a clock struck one.

I turned down the road beyond the bridge as a car was approaching. My hotel lay on the opposite side and subconsciously I remained on the left pavement waiting for the vehicle to pass. My mind was still attuned to the gaiety and laughter of the party and only gradually did the fact dawn upon me that no headlamps were flooding the road with light. Nor was the car making any effort to pass me. I glanced over my shoulder and saw a large saloon, its side lights staring, following slowly in my wake.

I stopped and spun round. The big car accelerated and drew level. A man's face from beneath the brim of a Homburg hat gleamed from an open window.

A voice—the accent familiar—spoke. "Are you Mr. Portway?"

I was fully alert now, my mind gripped by a nameless dread.

"Why?" I answered defensively.

The car door opened and the stranger emerged to face me. The driver, indistinguishable in the gloom, remained at the wheel.

The man put his hand into his breast pocket. So he was wearing a shoulder holster I thought and backed carefully towards the greater darkness. The tense atmosphere of tri-power-controlled Austria— "Third Man" and all—awoke within me.

He spoke again. "Take it easy," he said and handed me a white card.

I took it warily and tried to see the writing. With difficulty I made out the words "United States Military Intelligence".

Some of my fright evaporated but I was still suspicious.

"What do you want?" I asked. Out of the corner of my eye I watched the man in the driving seat flick on a lighter for his cigar. The flame revealed a check shirt of vivid pattern. Unconsciously the driver had convinced me further of their bona-fides. No self-respecting Soviet agent would be seen dead in a thing like that.

"We want a few words with you, if you please," replied the man in the road, adding in a more informal manner, "come and sit in the car where it's warmer."

Hesitatingly I climbed into the back seat. They could have got me in by force anyway. The driver's companion joined him.

"We understand you are proposing to visit Summerau tomorrow morning," he glanced at the luminous dial of his watch, "No, sorry this morning." A ghost of a smile was on the man's face as he looked at me for confirmation.

It wasn't their business, but I saw no reason to deny it. I nodded.

"You know it's in the Ruski zone?" he went on.

"Yes." I was in one of my uncommunicative moods.

The American continued: "We have no authority to stop you, but very strongly advise you not to go."

Resentment boiled inside me. I replied primly, "much as I appreciate the concern of the United States, I simply cannot cancel my arrangements." I saw their looks of concern and realised I was being unnecessarily stubborn. I started to tell them the reasons for the journey.

"We know," the driver spoke for the first time.

I was nonplussed. I tried to fathom the various possible sources where the information could have been gained. There was my letter posted last night. And, of course, the telegram. In a place like Vienna one might as well paint it on the wall of St. Stephens. Even so, this bunch must have acted pretty fast.

"No good me asking how, I suppose?"

"No." It was their turn to be cagey.

I spent nearly half an hour in the car and the conversation got bogged down in a groove. The Americans tried every gambit to prevent my excursion and I solemnly and monotonously declared my intentions of going.

"Well, it's your funeral," was the driver's last word on the subject. "Like a lift back to your Expresso?"

I assented gladly. I could use a drink. Only as I watched the red rear lights disappearing into the night did it strike me that they must have been on my tail for some time. Fortunately my friends were still where I had left them, but wondering why it took me so long to go to the hotel and back. At the next port of call I tried to buy a round of wine, only to discover that I had not, after all, replenished my supply of cash, a situation which took a bit of explaining!

42

When finally I did make the hotel there was only time for a cat-nap as I had to be up again by five. It was not even worth undressing. Anyway the trains that ran past the back of the building made quite sure I did not oversleep.

A bright sky offered the promise of a fine day as I hurried along the empty streets towards the station. I felt fresh and determined in spite of the lack of sleep. Within two and a half hours, if all went well, I should be seeing Anna again. It was hard to refrain from running.

The central station was a modern airy building with an air of quiet efficiency. I had bought my ticket yesterday, so made my way straight to the buffet. Breakfasting on a *wurst* sandwich and steaming cup of coffee I spared a thought for Liverpool Street station at this hour of the morning!

Then I choked into my coffee. On the other side of the open grill doors of the first platform were the two American agents. They had not seen me and were engaged in conversation with a station official. The arrangement by which, Norman, on his way to work, would drive away my car from the hotel, so acting as a decoy had not worked. I shrugged. It mattered little anyway, except for the Americans' own peace of mind.

I reached my departure platform—number four—by the simple expedient of crossing the tracks when neither station staff or reception committee were looking. The Summerau train was in and a few early morning travellers were selecting seats. The destination board indicated it to be a slow '*personenzug*', stopping at all stations. By the central clock I checked my watch. Eight minutes to go.

Four had gone when a trio of faces appeared at the window. Two of them I knew. "Good morning, Mr. Portway," said the one with the jazzy line in shirts.

"Good morning to you," I replied, "couldn't you sleep either?"

Ignoring my friendly taunt he introduced me to the third member of the party. He was older, wore a light mackintosh and did not look American.

"This is Inspector Salzbach of the Austrian Police," he said, "we have news for you."

"Oh yes," I replied without enthusiasm, nodding to the policeman.

Unabashed the American continued, "The Inspector's district includes the frontier at Summerau. His men at Summerau station reported a couple of hours ago that three agents of the Soviet Security

Police are waiting there for the expected arrival of an Englishman. Of course, it might be another Englishman, but I don't see what Summerau has to draw trainloads of Englishmen in the early morning." He looked at me quizzically.

I still refused to be deterred from my purpose. It was too incredible that the Intelligence organisations of two world powers should be mobilised to catch one little man going to visit his girl.

"How do I know you're telling the truth?" I countered.

For an answer the Inspector showed me a cable reply form. The writing was in German, but it looked authentic. I continued to hesitate. Yet they had a strong point in the very incredulousness of the situation. Only a fool would make up a story like that and these men weren't fools.

The other American saw my hesitation. He shot another bolt.

"Last night you asked us how we knew all about you and your girl," he said quietly. "In Vienna you sent her a telegram, didn't you, and a postcard from Zagreb? You gave everybody plenty of warning."

A whistle blew, doors slammed. But I was off that train as if it were red hot.

"Thanks a lot," I murmured to the two smiling Americans. I decided I rather liked them.

They, in their turn, must have seen my crestfallen look. "Come and have a real breakfast," they suggested.

Back in the station buffet we had waffles, fried eggs and, since Americans don't require a reason for anything, champagne. This time my mind was far too engrossed to take in Liverpool Street.

Our first broken tryst was a bitter disappointment to me. I thought of the slight figure of Anna waiting wide-eyed on a strange hostile border; waiting for a man who never came. The fact that it was I who had let her down made it worse. To break a date was a woman's prerogative.

For three days I remained in Linz. They were days of torture as I worried myself sick as to how Anna had fared at Horni Dvoriste, but they were also days of fun for Norman saw to it that I had little time for sorrow.

I found a reluctance to leave as I took the Salzburg road en route for home. My rebuff had crystallised into a cold defeat, but it was a defeat that acted as a buttress to my determination to succeed next time. Already my mind was a jump ahead planning fresh assaults.

Only later did I discover that Anna had never received a telegram or letter from Vienna. The Zagreb picture postcard reached her, however, its contents being carefully noted by both the Czech Security Police and British Counter-Intelligence, not to mention the other interested parties. Everyone, it seemed, appeared to be enjoying my correspondence. Everyone, too, was making very certain that I never reached my fiancee.

CHAPTER 5

The Fair Guest of Leipzig

By Easter 1954 nine months had elapsed since my ill-fated Austrian episode. Nine months of wearisome argument with the Embassies of Eastern Europe. Countless attempts to obtain an entry visa for Czechoslovakia, or even a neighbouring People's Republic had met with a firm refusal or frustrating silence. The dice were heavily loaded against me, but for Anna, whose marriage application had been curtly rejected, the dice became dynamite.

My relatives and friends shook their heads. "It's hopeless", they told me kindly, "give it up and find a nice English girl instead". But I only smiled and heeded not their advice. There was something wrong in the world, something rotten, when the government of a state refused the simple right of its citizens to choose whom they marry. It was bad enough their being forbidden to cross its frontiers, but the meddling in the private lives of those folk who chose to find happiness outside them was the very basis of slavery.

In spite of my anger I did not allow this aspect of the business to rule my mind. The outlook to me was very much simpler. I loved Anna and she loved me. We had decided to become husband and wife and to find happiness in life together. The fact that Anna was harder to get than most other girls made not the slightest difference to the issue. And if the state reckoned it could quench the romance it could think again.

It was in this frame of mind that this following Easter — the anniversary of our engagement—I again left the United Kingdom to repeat the successful expedition of the previous year to Cheb. With a five-day holiday it seemed as good a way of spending it as any and I had an idea they hadn't changed the border regulations. They could hardly have expected me to return, though I wouldn't place high odds on my making it a third time. Ten days previously I had written Anna a letter telling her in phrases only she could recognise—for I did not require the company of a European intelligence network—of my intended movements that Eastertide. I received the acknowledgment the morning I left.

It worked a treat. The regulations had not changed; nor indeed had the S.N.B. officer on duty at Cheb station. He all but threw a fit when I turned up again visa-less but triumphant on the arm of a radiant fiancee. But the triumph was short-lived. Again the cold shadow of despair hung over us as we clung to one another before the inevitable parting. Then and there I took a vow that next time it would be more than just a fleeting appointment at a railway station.

The chance to keep my vow materialised that autumn. At home, shortly after my return, an advertisement in a newspaper caught my eye and held it like a magnet. There before me was a key to one small door in the blank wall of frustration. It was an announcement of the forthcoming re-opening, after a sixteen year interval, of the International Trade Fair at Leipzig.

With the aid of a map of East Germany I began there and then to hatch another scheme. Here at last was a chink in the Iron Curtain to be exploited to the full. Once in East Germany, within the enemy's camp, so to speak, anything could happen.

The necessary documents required to visit the Fair were surprisingly easy to obtain. A Fair card, obtainable for a few shillings through my own firm ensured, with unbelievable alacrity, an impressive Soviet visa bristling with stamps, "CCCPs" and hieroglyphics. A Piccadilly travel agency made the arrangements for the journey which included the substantial fare reduction offered to business visitors using the East German State Railway, and reserved for me lodgings for four nights through the Leipzig private house boarding scheme. This supplemented the sparse hotel accommodation availability and, as well as being cheaper, the prospect of living with a private household appealed to me since I had no desire to come under the eyes of Communist hotel staff.

While these preparations were under way I had been carrying on an involved correspondence with Anna in what, I hoped, she would recognise as a simple code. The first letter told her of my intention to visit the Leipzig Fair that September and gave dates and details including a suggested meeting place outside one of the Fair gates. I had wrapped up the instructions in a fable concerning a dog and my first reply made it clear that the message had fallen upon stony ground. Exasperated, I read of a sweet little suggestion concerning dachshund puppies! Later missives met with more success as Anna got the message and responded in kind.

She made it clear from the start, however, that there was little hope of her being allowed to visit the Fair or even neighbouring Communist territory. Being no longer employed she could hardly find the slightest excuse of a commercial nature to attend a trade exhibition of any description. Furthermore, her rejected foreign marriage application had aroused the interest of the secret police and they would have very good reasons to ensure that she stayed at home.

I was hardly surprised at these tidings and planned accordingly. We would meet at Decin, the Czech border town near the East German-Czech frontier. I gave her a date and said I would meet her there sometime that day. What I could not—dared not—tell her was a scheme within a scheme I had hatched for extracting her from Czechoslovak territory by way of the river Elbe, Bad Schandau and overland to Berlin. At that time, 1954, there was no Wall and passage between east and west sectors was less strictly controlled. It took all my ingenuity to write of the Decin meeting arrangements and by the time we had done with it the canine anthology was wearing a little thin.

As the day of my departure drew nearer so I accumulated a treasure trove of information on conditions and security habits prevalent in the German Democratic Republic. Letters to West German friends, close examination of newspapers, periodicals and intelligence digests, contacts with acquaintances who had driven through the Soviet zone in recent months or who had once holiday'd in "Saxon Switzerland" between Dresden and the Czech border. All my gleanings I filed away for reference. Perhaps the most valuable snippet of knowledge was some information on the flow strength, depth and composition of the bed of the Elbe at Bad Schandau which I collected from a nameless individual in a Wapping pub. My informant was also able to make some revealing suggestions concerning the barge traffic in the area.

The four days I would remain in Leipzig would not be wasted. I had no doubt that many of the city's inhabitants could be encouraged to talk and where there was talk there was at least one pair of ears very willing to listen. From these captives of their own land I hoped to complete my private dossier which would have to suffice as our bible for a one-way pilgrimage.

Dover took on an unusually homely look as "S.S. Invicta" slipped her moorings and slid smoothly out of the harbour. Turning my gaze to the quietly heaving murkiness of a September sea I pondered on the journey ahead. If Leipzig seemed a long way to go, it was likely soon to seem a much longer way back.

A prominent notice on a currency exchange kiosk on Helmstedt station shouted "Obtain your East German marks here at favourable rates". Five kilometres down the line at Marienborn, all East German marks found on travellers entering the German Democratic Republic were promptly impounded together with their owners if German.

Between these two blatant contradictions lay another frontier as lethal as any between East and West. Making it particularly obnoxious was the fact that it was German staring at German across the ploughed strip. No communication existed, informal or otherwise, and where mercy had died only hate survived.

I had to change trains at Magdeburg. By choosing a later connection I gained my first impression of life in the other Germany and did not like what I saw. In the Federal territories a war ruin was becoming a rarity, a thing to be looked at and remarked upon. In Magdeburg that warm and sunny afternoon I found myself back in the Germany of 1946, to a country of fire-ravaged ruin and bleak despair.

Mellowed by time and partly screened by immense propaganda posters, the ruins were less conspicuous perhaps, but the despair remained. It showed in the empty shop windows, the long food queues, the poor quality of clothing worn and, most of all, in the eyes of the citizens themselves. I was glad to return to my train.

There was a long, unscheduled wait at Halle while a check on papers by the "People's Police" was made. The usual delay followed while my passport was read and re-read.

"You are on the wrong train," I was told.

"This goes to Leipzig?"

"Yes," said the man, "but it is not for auslanders."

I asked if a colour bar existed in the G.D.R.* but fortunately he did not understand. Instead he went on at me in a spate of German and, using an old P.o.W. subterfuge, I pretended not to understand. The policeman gave it up as a bad job and stalked off to find easier prey. I'd committed my first offence.

It was easy to see why the train was not for the eyes of foreigners. The coaches would have shamed even British Railways. In addition a non-stop blast of martial music varied by shouted quotations from Karl Marx and Lenin was piped into every compartment, and it couldn't be turned off. Together with my fellow passengers I suffered in silence.

Late in the afternoon we arrived at Leipzig. The solid walls of the station had been gaily bedecked with flags of all nations and I noticed that the authorities had deemed it prudent to repair this particular building. Even so, the glass roof was entirely missing though this was not noticeable until it rained.

*German Democratic Republic

My first objective was the foreign visitors' centre at the Neues Rathaus, or new town hall, where registration, currency exchange and accommodation allotment was reputed to be carried out. On the way I took my time, sampling the atmosphere of the city and peering with interest into shop windows. Though shoddy to Western eyes it was obvious that considerable efforts had been made to make the place attractive to its influx of foreign visitors. The shops themselves were reasonably well stocked, even if most of their wares were in the display windows, the streets were suspiciously tidy, the trams freshly painted, and the traffic a lot denser than had been the case of Magdeburg. Many of the private vehicles were of non-German origin, and the citizens of Leipzig gave the game away by crowding round to gaze in awe at any stationary American car. Much rebuilding had been carried out and not a ruin could be seen near the city centre.

I dropped into a small *gasthaus* at the corner of the market place for a beer and it was not until I had half emptied my glass that I remembered I only held coupons for exchange into *ostmarks* and no East German currency itself. The proprietor was in no way put out, however, offering me the drink on the house. This provided us both with an excuse for conversation from which it emerged that he was not an enthusiastic supporter of the regime. "See all this here," he finished, pointing at the street, "all fake and show. The day after the Fair ends all the stock in the shops, all the food especially imported into the restaurants, even most of the German cars in the streets, will all disappear. Do you know they've even imported people here just for exhibition." The man spat the words into his own beer.

The Neues Rathaus turned out to be pretty old Rathaus, but with typical Teutonic thoroughness it had been turned into a very efficient visitors' reception centre. In a series of booths the visitor was documentated, tagged and classified under the benevolent gaze of President Wilhelm Pieck, whose photograph was a compulsory pin-up in every office. A form was required to be completed at each booth and sheaves of instructions, rules and regulations were given in exchange. Cynically I read the message of welcome received from the immigration authority. It was in four languages and after bidding the "Dear Fair Guest from Abroad" successful business with the "peace industry of the German Democratic Republic", the missive went on: "Should there be any necessity for you to travel further on to some other place in the Republic in connection with your Fair business, or perhaps for private reasons, you have the opportunity of applying to the Ministry of Foreign Affairs to have your visa extended. We beg you to be kind enough to observe these directions as your present visa is only valid for the Fair town of Leipzig". Somehow I didn't think my private reasons for leaving the "Fair town" would entitle me to another visa from the Ministry of Foreign Affairs, so I would save them the trouble.

The Deutsche Notenbank cold-bloodedly robbed me with an official rate of exchange that made the toughest of "Fair guests" wince and handed out yet another slip of paper, listing the penalties for an impressive variety of possible currency irregularities. Finally a coldly aloof young lady in the neighbouring chamber gave me the address of my accommodation—which was payable in advance. I then had to go through most of the proceedings again, for having duly paid, it was necessary to return to the Deutsche Notenbank again for further funds.

My accommodation card gave the name "Frau Lindener, Brand-vorwerkstrasse 80/1". I turned to the back to see what state punishments were in store for "Fair guests" who snored or smoked in bed, but was disappointed. I asked the aloof young *Deutches madchen* how I got to Brandvorwerkstrasse and decided it was a silly question for I was directed to another booth!

Outside the station I found the main tram terminus where I learnt a Number 5 tram would take me most of the way. But I forgot to ask the direction and ended up in the wrong end of the city. Having completed a circuit of the Leipzig tramway system I finally reached the district I wanted, but even then only made Brandvorwerkstrasse with the help of an obliging citizen.

The Lindeners were a charming couple. Together with their small daughter they lived on the first floor of a block of terraced flats indistinguishable from others in the same street. Frau Lindener, a woman in her early thirties, made me most genuinely welcome right from the start, insisting that once across their threshold, I became automatically one of the family. Both she and her husband, a thin, studious intellectual, who played something in the Leipzig Symphony Orchestra, spoke good English, and before long the mischievous little offspring was fast making up, with me as teacher, for a neglected English education.

80/1 Brandvorwerkstrasse became very much a home from home for me that evening and the Lindeners were unstinting in their hospitality. I wondered how much they got of my "accommodation remittance" after state deductions, but did not allow this to spoil a hefty appetite.

51

I rose early the next morning and, following Herr Lindener's precise instructions, reached the Fair ground as it opened. Entering by the west gate and showing my pass to a battery of policemen, I found myself in a world of politics and commercialism. The place of honour went, of course, to the Soviet Union whose giant palace, topped by a blood red star of ludicrous dimensions, made the centre piece of the Fair. The German Democratic Republic as host came a poor second, followed closely by the pagoda-like pavilion of the People's Republic of China. Poland, Czechoslovakia, Rumania, Hungary, Bulgaria and Albania, in a supporting role, defiantly tried to show off a flash of their individual national characteristics beneath their yoke of hammer, sickle and red star that the dull uniformity of Communism decreed. Further, much further down the line, came the "neutral" countries of India, Argentina, Chile, Turkey, Peru and the Arab States. Crowded out of all proportion to their size, the single pavilion housing the few exhibits of France, Belgium and Great Britain was tucked away in a corner. By accident or design it was next door to the lavatories.

At midday I found myself scanning the crowd of onlookers outside the east gate in case, by some miracle, Anna had been able to reach the original rendezvous. Two Russian soldiers with tommy guns eyed me curiously. I told myself I was not disappointed: that I knew she wouldn't be there. But I had not the strength of purpose to believe my own lie.

Tiring of the Fair ground in the afternoon, I caught a tram into town. My first call was at the office of the Czechoslovak Legation. I trotted out my "spiel" in support of an entry visa required for sudden urgent business with the Czech state engineering concern in Prague. There was no harm in trying.

I need not have bothered. "Come back in a week," said a horrid little man in a loud suit. "We may have an answer then." No doubt they would, I mused, but hardly one worth coming back for.

I next went to the railway station to enquire about tickets to the Czech border. "Have you a travel permit?" asked the booking clerk, his eyes narrowing. I looked blankly at him. "All travellers in the G.D.R. must be in possession of a police permit to move further than fifty kilometres from their place of residence." "Furthermore," went on the clerk warming to his subject, "all foreigners must have a visa to visit any part of the Republic other than Leipzig." "Anything else?" I asked weakly. Re-animated, the man continued, "only the small matter of visiting a frontier district. This also requires a police permit; unless of course you were in transit to Czechoslovakia."

"When I've got all these permits do I come back to you?"

The clerk pondered the question. "No," he replied, looking round. "Firstly, only travel agencies can issue tickets for journeys of over fifty kilometres and secondly, I'd have died of old age before you collected all those permits!"

Undaunted, I sought the office of the State Travel Bureau, only to find it closed. A belated lunch at a State-run "H.O."* restaurant, where the surrender of food coupons produced a meal of very inferior quality, ended my activities for the day. Wending my way homewards I made a detour to pass the east gate of the Fair just in case......

The following morning I girded my loins for battle and descended upon police headquarters. "A permit to move freely in the G.D.R." "Why? You wish to go to Prague? Then may we please see your Czech visa? No visa? But one is applied for? Well, come back when you have it and we shall be delighted to issue the permit."

I tried a different approach. "A visit to Bad Schandau? But that's a military zone and you'll require a permit from the People's Army." I got the point. The People's Army—even if I found the right department—would no doubt swing it all back to the police and the game of snakes and ladders would start all over again. They had it all nicely buttoned up without having to lose face with an unconditional "No".

The Travel Bureau office was open when I got there. "I want to get to Prague the day after tomorrow," I began in a no-nonsense tone.

The elderly assistant behind the counter was apologetic. "We can only issue tickets to the border," he said.

"That will do. I can get another one at Decin."

"You have a visa to travel presumably?"

"Of course."

"May I see your passport please, sir, so that the required information can be entered on the ticket application form."

Holding my ground I handed over the book. The man peered at the maze of stamps in obvious bewilderment. "Which—".

"That one," I hissed as if disgusted at his ignorance and jabbed my finger on the Soviet hieroglyphics. The poor old chap looked embarrassed and I hated myself. He wrote something down on a form.

"If you would come back tomorrow morning, sir, your tickets will be ready."

I thanked him nonchalantly, retrieved my passport and left on a carpet of air. I had found a chink in the armour. Admittedly it was only one skittle down, but another good bowl and the lot would come

*Handel's Organisation

53

tumbling. A nasty idea nagged me that other eyes would see the tickets before I got them; hence the delay in their issue. I shrugged my shoulders. Sufficient unto the day is the evil thereof—.

Returning to the Fair by way of the east gate and an optimistic perusal of the small crowd that surrounded it, I dutifully made another tour of the stands. The Chinese pavilion was full of tea, carpets and Mao Tse-Tung, East Germany exhibited a natty range of Leica photographic equipment which was repeated in the West German pavilion, since, as well as two Germany's there were also two Leica combines. Yugoslavia showed her prowess with plums and cherries, India had much in common with her arch-enemy China, except that for Mao read Nehru. But the biggest crowds were congregated in the small building near the lavatories where France, Belgium and Britain combined to give a tantalising glimpse of the fruits of capitalism. Hundreds of people stood gaping at a Rolls Royce and the latest Paris fashions.

The third day started well. Presenting myself at the Travel Bureau I was handed my rail tickets together with detailed information regarding time of departure and arrival, and change of trains at Dresden. My stock of *ostmarks* took a nose-dive in return. In an effort to save precious currency I went without lunch though the distractions of the Fair were hardly strong enough to compensate, throughout the afternoon, for an unsatisfied appetite. After a final East gate vigil I returned to the Lindeners who, bless them, laid on a special last night supper.

Early next morning, in a misty drizzle, I boarded the Dresden-bound express and settled myself in the corner of a compartment as far away from a loudspeaker as possible. Against a brass band polka I thought of Anna probably now arriving at Decin. I thought that I must love her very much to do what I intended to do. I thought that she would have to love me very much to agree to accompany me on the journey I intended for us.

The express existed in name only. It dawdled contentedly across the undulating terrain stopping when and where the fancy took it. The polka gave way to a reedy voice rhapsoding the joy of living in a Communist state protected by the ever vigilant and mighty Soviet Union: a point of view that was not reflected in the stony faces of my travelling companions. Relays of ticket inspectors marked, punched and tore bits of my ticket at nearly every stop and I hoped there would be enough of it left by the time I reached the border.

Shortly after the bustle of Meissen station had been left behind the door slid open to admit both a ticket inspector and a policeman,

Automatically, as if jerked by hidden strings, the puppets of the People's Paradise reached for their papers. Expecting the worst I watched the minion of the law browse through my passport. His eyes alighted on my Soviet visa and to my amazement he snapped to attention, saluted and gravely handed me back the book. For a full minute I studied the signature on the visa trying to identify the scrawl as that of the great protector himself, J. Stalin!

At Dresden main station I left the train in search of the connection. Straightaway I ran into another police check at the barrier. There were three of them this time and they looked as if they knew their business. I waited, subdued and watchful, ready for the outburst. Instead I got guard-of-honour treatment. They all saluted and took considerable pains to direct me to the platform of the Prague express. Given another few seconds in my august presence I think they would have presented arms!

Truly I had found the key to the golden gate.

CHAPTER 6

Saxon Skirmish

The face of Dresden still wore the dreadful scars of the heaviest bombing raid in history. I had momentarily seen this beautiful city in 1944 unscathed by war but the tragedy it suffered early the following year left it a burnt shell. It also provided the regime that followed Hitler's with a telling propaganda weapon and from every wall and hoarding the silent invective leered. As the cultural capital of the G.D.R. it was high on the building priority list and the huge blocks of flats rising in the suburbs competed with the reconstruction of historic buildings and monuments. I stood on the old *Augustusbrucke* over the Elbe which separates the new town from the old. The silhouette of the *Altstadt* towers reminded me of Prague.

Returning to the station and giving a pair of Russian military policemen a wide berth I boarded the Berlin-Prague Express. This was, if appearances were anything to go by, a crack train: an impressive thing of silver and black. Even the third class compartments were of the "soft" variety for which my tattered ticket showed I had paid a substantial supplement. I watched Dresden fade from view as the train entered the woods that hugged the foothills of the Erzgebirge.

Within half an hour we were clattering into Bad Schandau. Though more than five kilometres from the frontier this pleasant spa resort was the centre for customs and immigration. Alone in my spacious compartment I awaited events.

There being few travellers for Czechoslovakia the immigration authorities came through the train like a dose of salts.

"To where are you going, sir?" the official asked following the usual prolonged examination of my passport.

"Prague," I replied with the new born optimism.

Another silence, then: "Have you a current Czech visa?"

"The Soviet Embassy in London gave me the permission necessary." I tapped the magic stamp impatiently.

Plainly uneasy the official left. Two minutes later he was back with a large police officer in tow.

It all began again. "May I see your passport, please?"

I handed it over.

"Why no Czech visa?" he asked obviously worried by a deficiency that no amount of alternative documentation could cover.

"No time," I lied, "I learnt I had to go to Prague on business the day before I left for the Leipzig Fair."

The police officer was adamant. "You must have a Czech visa," he persisted. "If you return to Berlin immediately you could still reach Prague tomorrow."

I turned on my indignant act. "But I must reach Prague tonight. I have an important appointment in the morning. Don't you see—."

" I am sorry but you have not the correct papers and I cannot let you go further."

The man's tone was final and when it came to an argument about the validity of papers with a German I knew when I was beaten. One might as well talk to a brick wall.

The chap was still uneasy, however, as he escorted me, politely prattling on about the necessity of sticking to regulations, to a waiting northbound train standing in a siding. Already it was quite full although not due to leave for another half an hour.

The officer saluted, wished me a *gute Reise* and departed. I gave him five minutes and likewise left. Dodging round the locomotive at the head of the train I approached the exit alert for signs of my police-man friend or for any authority other than railway staff at the barrier. The customs and immigration section of the station lay at the further end and I was glad to note that this was where most of the police were congregated.

At the barrier I gave up my ticket. In a moment I would be out in the town and away from the eyes of authority. I would make my own way to the border and still make Decin in time to meet Anna. The border would not be all that heavily guarded; in fact the outward journey would be a good rehearsal for our return together. In military parlance, a "dry run".

"Your passport, please." The well-worn words cut into my excited deliberations.

A young policeman emerged from an open doorway his face a question mark of suspicion.

I cursed under my breath. Why hadn't I found a more unorthodox exit? It would have been easy and nobody would have been any the wiser. I turned to humour my new tormentor.

He flipped through the pages of my passport and seemed satisfied.

"Where are you going?"

"For a walk around."

"A walk around what?"

"Oh, just across the road." A silly question deserved a silly answer. I added: "Actually, I'm waiting for my train."

"Where is your destination?"

"Prague." Very nearly I had said "Berlin."

The ticket collector had been listening to the scintillating exchange. He added his voice.

"The Prague train leaves in seven minutes."

The policeman decided to be helpful. "Come along then, quick." He propelled me back into the station proper after retrieving my ticket from the collector. Hustling me on to a first class coach he saluted and withdrew.

I took refuge in a corner seat sinking into the luxurious cushions. Hiding my face in my hands I pretended to be asleep. Having been already expelled from this train I had no desire to meet any former acquaintances.

In spite of my anti-social behaviour I was not to avoid the eagle eye of a roving ticket inspector. Full of zeal he descended upon me.

Of course my ticket and my seat were not compatible. Would I, please, remove my personage to a lower standard of habitation. Without demur I moved into the corridor and along it into the adjoining coach. And then I came face to face with the police inspector.

There was a bellow of rage.

"What are you doing on this train again?"

"One of your men put me on it," I blandly replied.

"Why didn't you stay on the other train?"

"I was looking for a toilet."

The inspector saw that he was getting nowhere. He pursed his lips, glared at me and said: "Come with me." All efforts at politeness had evaporated.

In silence I was led out of the station passing the policeman whose helpful motives had got me into the latest jam. I pretended not to see him. A small barracks adjoined the station forecourt, the entrance guarded by a Russian soldier. He took little notice of us as we entered. The inspector knocked at a door in a dark passage.

Inside, sitting behind a table strewn with papers, was a Russian captain. The inspector saluted him and in a spate of German explained, as best he could, the situation. The Russian listened bewildered but not seriously concerned.

The inspector finished and the captain turned to me. In passable English he said: "I hear you had trouble with a lavatory."

It was my turn to look bewildered. The captain explained. "This man here tells me you prefer southbound lavatories to northbound ones!" His young good-looking features relaxed into a grin.

I found myself liking this Russian but was fast losing faith in the magic powers of my visa. Presumably even Russian soldiers have to read a little before they become captains. Presumably, too, they could read their own language even if nobody else could. I wanted to kick the German as he handed over my passport.

"This is a permit for the town of Leipzig only," said the captain tapping my visa, "You are about two hundred kilometres off course."

I switched to a new track. "When foreigners come to the British Industries Fair they are not expected to remain in Birmingham."

"This isn't England," snapped the inspector. He made England sound like a dirty word.

I said nothing. Sometimes silence is truly golden.

The Russian and the German conferred. I followed some of the conversation. The gist of it seemed to be that neither the Red Army or the German People's Police wanted the responsibility of my apprehension. I was nobody's baby. The Russian eventually won on a technical point and anyway he was the boss.

"Can I go now?" I asked helpfully offering what seemed to be a sensible solution.

All I got for my pains was another snarl and the pronouncement that I could go nowhere since I was under arrest.

"Why?" My indignant howl echoed round the small room. If I had a sneaking regard for the Russian officer it stopped very short of this fat Commie kraut.

It was the Russian, however, who supplied the answer.

"For choosing the wrong lavatory!" he said ushering us out of the room.

Returning to the station I was made to wait in a police office amongst a dozen of the inspector's men. One of them gave me a glass of beer and, as soon as the inspector had gone, they became the friendliest of souls.

A whistle blew and in company with four heavily-armed men I was hustled, to my delighted surprise, back again on to the Prague Express. The good Lord above, I thought, must be as determined as I to get me on that train. With considerable satisfaction I watched the vulture of a ticket inspector glare at me and pass by. As befitted our combined status my escort and I had a reserved first class compartment to ourselves!

The train had hardly gathered speed before having to stop again at a small wayside halt shadowed by the tall cliffs forming one wall of the Elbe valley. A drizzle from a gloomy sky had set in partly obscuring the magnificent scenery but, as only my escort and I left the train, I could see the river meandering through the wide gorge. Even as I looked a string of barges moved steadily downstream.

"*Tschechoslowakei!*" announced the senior member of my escort pointing to a jetty that projected into the river.

I managed to keep the interest out of my voice as I replied "Oh, yes," though my heart was pounding at my ribs. Just a mile upstream my Anna would be patiently waiting. So near and yet. .

Across the tracks a well worn footpath lead us over a damp meadow to the west bank of the river. On several occasions I enquired where we were going but could evince no satisfactory response. But the nearer I could legally get to Decin the better. After all if a police escort chose to come my way who was I to stop them.

From close at hand I could see that the river was not the sluggish thing it looked from the train. A fast current stirred the grey waters whipping up little plumes of froth. A police launch tried to drag its anchor as we boarded it from another jetty just fifty yards from Czech territory. With ill-concealed interest I watched a northbound barge heave to at the Czech control point for, presumably, customs examination.

The little launch chugged bravely upstream cleaving a diagonal course across the river. Every second brought us nearer the other jetty. My eyes were rivetted on the stationary barge for signs of a search but could see nothing.

We disembarked at a step in the opposite bank and acting for all the world like a party of school kids made our way to a cluster of houses. In spite of the merriment I closely studied my environment gauging distances, the available cover and the general situation. I didn't think there'd be a heavy traffic in "wet backs"*. It was too

*Illegal river border crossers.

much a case of out of the frying pan into a fire.

The hamlet had been cleared of its civilian population and the big villas, which once must have formed a capitalist stronghold, were unkempt and shuttered. Save for police and soldiers the place was deserted and wore the air of a front line village in war. We stopped at a villa, that, although shuttered, was occupied.

In a bare reception room I was offered a chair at a rough wooden table and a cold meal of rye bread and liver sausage, together with a litre jug of beer, was brought to me. I was hungry and made short work of it. While finishing my beer a police officer joined me and put me through a mild form of interrogation. In spite of his ardent views on Communism he was not an unpleasant fellow though I could not make out whether his questions were prompted by duty or simple curiosity. Whenever I could get a question in myself I tried to find out about my immediate future.

Then I had a brainwave. "I have a friend at Decin. Do you think I might telephone her?" I asked innocently. At least I could speak to Anna and assure her I was close at hand.

The officer wanted to know who she was.

"Oh, just a girl friend," I said, like the sailor who had a girl in every port.

"We'll see about it," replied the man. His tone told me that he wouldn't.

My next visitor was the jovial Russian captain. We greeted one another like long lost brothers. I was bombarded with questions from him, too, but they certainly were not the sort that arose from line of duty. The Dean of Canterbury, Stratford-on-Avon, Field Marshal Montgomery. All came up for a verbal airing. I again managed to insert my question concerning Anna.

"We'll see about it," came the answer in the same unconvincing manner. He showed even less interest than the German.

The villa was a police barracks of sorts and following the departure of the Russian captain an assortment of policemen trooped in to try out their even more limited English. It was highly bewildering and when one of them invited me to a film show about to commence in their canteen I was pleased to accept. At least it would be a rest from answering daft questions. The hour-long celluloid epic concerned the activities of a Soviet Hero of Labour. Personally I would have preferred Superman and by the time the comrade hero had sacrificed home, girl-friend and holiday for the sake of a steel furnace I was very ready

61

for more questioning. Paroxysms of clapping from its audience brought the film to a close though this undeserved appreciation was probably more for the benefit of the Russian captain.

Towards evening the drizzle ceased and the sun broke through the heavy clouds. I asked permission for a walk and to my surprise got it. Accompanied by a young N.C.O. hardly out of his teens I made a tour of the village. At the actual border we came across a troop of armoured cars, their 20 mm. guns pointing ominously into Czechoslovakia. Barbed wire barricades sealed the approaches to German territory. Down the road, under a red, white and blue Czech flag, similar warlike preparations were in evidence.

"Expecting an invasion?" I enquired of my guide.

The N.C.O. looked at me to see if I was being funny. "Just normal security," was the cold reply. He didn't look the laughing boy type.

Trusting lot of bastards, I thought.

Dusk was upon us when we returned to the villa. I began to worry about how long Anna would remain at Decin. All day I had said. I hadn't mentioned night. I tried again with my phone call request and at last succeeded in obtaining a reply even if it was negative. I dared not press the point too hard in case they became nosey about Anna.

The Russian captain, all dolled up in breeches and jackboots, came in to bid his farewells and impart the information that I was to be returned to Berlin. Hardly had I collected my scattered thoughts to channel them into a plan of action when my four original policemen entered. They said I was to "*komm mit*". Back on the express to Berlin the operation would be doomed. It would have to be crash action...

I asked if I could go to the toilet before leaving. But there was no escape that way. The window was boarded up except for a slit at the top and removal would require a battering ram.

We took a different route back to the river. Reaching its bank at the nearest point we followed the hurrying waters towards Czech territory. The tow-path was muddy and slippery. I noticed that it led close to a belt of trees that projected from the woods clothing the eastern slopes of the valley. Past that and we should be back to where the launch was moored. The wood was the only chance.

Looking ahead I tried to plot the position of the shortest points between path and trees. We walked in silence I being too preoccupied for light conversation. In front of me an N.C.O. armed only with an automatic pistol in a holster led the way. The other three were strung out behind but only the nearest constituted a danger. He had a machine carbine, unloaded, for it carried no magazine.

If I could get to those trees before the shooting started there was a sporting chance of my reaching Czech territory. I'd have to keep off the roads, of course, but I had the river and the valley to guide me. Anna might have left Decin station by the time I got there. If so, I was prepared even to hump it to her home. My stubborn streak was showing again.

We neared the spot I had chosen for the getaway. I gave the man behind me ten seconds to recover from the shock, unsling his weapon, clip on a magazine from his belt, cock the mechanism and open fire. I thought I could be safe in the trees inside of eight. The N.C.O. might be faster but I could only pray that he was not a crack pistol shot.

The path made a curve and some undergrowth momentarily hid the two policemen behind me. We were still a few yards from my designated point of departure but it was an opportunity too good to miss.

I took a deep breath and hurled myself sideways. Exactly three steps I managed and then the ground came up to meet me violently. That rabbit hole or whatever was hidden in grass and moss probably saved my life. Winded I lay there and watched my escort rush towards me very much alert. It struck me that I had underestimated their quickness of draw by about four seconds.

"*Was ist los?*" The N.C.O.'s voice sounded more alarmed than angry.

"I was after a lizard, a lovely yellow green specimen with spots," I babbled on to allay the tension. No doubt they did not understand but no matter just as long as they had no serious suspicions of my real intentions.

"*Komm*," the command was cold and as we covered the remaining distance to the boat I noticed the man behind me no longer carried an unloaded gun...

There was no tourist atmosphere as we chugged back across the Elbe. No longer were the sights pointed out to me; nor was I given place of honour in the boat. Miserably I looked back across the foaming wake to the Czech pier receding into the distance.

I was pointedly locked in the guardroom of the border post station. Gloomily I surveyed the faded silhouettes of British and American tanks that adorned the wall. 'Know your enemy', read the German caption. Over the window were iron bars.

Eventually I was released from my cell and allowed to sit in a room together with half a dozen frontier policemen. They were a friendly bunch and even my recent escort soon dropped their frigidness.

It was quite dark when I was taken outside again. A lone Vopo* carrying a briefcase accompanied me on the short timber platform.

"Are you coming too?" I asked him.

He nodded. Bells rang and a green light turned to red.

"We are stopping it just for you," he added referring to the Prague-Berlin Express, audibly approaching. They were making quite sure of getting me off their backs this time.

The silver diesel locomotive screeched to an unaccustomed halt at the little platform and together we boarded a first class compartment. Only the best for Leipzig businessmen I ruminated but I was not in a humorous mood. My business had still not been successfully concluded.

My companion and I spoke little on the journey. About the only prolonged exchange we had was when I was asked to contribute to my fare. I declined to do so on the grounds that I had no wish to go to Berlin in the first place and, more to the point, because I had no money. Ticket collectors came and went but my escort's pass kept them at bay. I was hardly an asset to the State Railway of the German Democratic Republic which at least gave me slight satisfaction. At the Berlin-Ring, the artificial frontier that encircles the city, squads of police probed under the seats in the accustomed manner prior to or following contamination with Western freedom.

In the cold early hours of the morning the express drew into the Ost-Bahnhof. I insisted upon my tame Vopo accompanying me through the barrier to save complications with the ticket collector. Only then did I release him and walk out alone into the dark, bisected city.

What was left of the night I spent in a small hotel in the Western sector where I would get better value for my dwindling reserves of cash. I marvelled at the ease of crossing by U-Bahn† the boundary line which, alas, was soon to be replaced by a wall marking the most deadly frontier in the world.

I returned to the Eastern sector next morning for one last fling. With some difficulty I located the Czech Consulate amongst the maze

*Colloquialism of Volkspolizei — People's Police.
†Underground railway system.

of drab streets. Even before the equally drab little man in the ill-cut suit opened his mouth in response to my optimistic visa application I knew the words of the litany: "Come back in about ten days and we'll have an answer from Prague." I gave the man a withering look and left.

Tired and depressed I returned to my hotel. Tomorrow I would return homewards with another failure to chalk up on my personal score-board. In the solitude of my room my thoughts were full of the small figure who waited on bleak railway stations for a fiance who never came. Again I had not kept the rendezvous. Again I had failed her. Again our hopes had soared and died.

CHAPTER 7

Magyar Mission

The most intriguing items in the big old-fashioned hotel bedroom were the bell-pushes. Three wooden knobs protruded from a neat frame against which, in diagram form, was the explanation of each bell. A second means of summoning servility was vested in the tasseled cords that hung languidly from a cracked plaster ceiling.

I eyed these gadgets with interest as slowly I changed for dinner. With the donning of my jacket I could resist the temptation no longer. Selecting the knob alongside the symbol for Chambermaid I pulled. If a bell ever rang somewhere in the bowels of the hotel it was never answered. The "Boots" and "Coachman" were equally reticent, so, getting into my stride I attacked the tasseled cord with immediate results. Together with the cord a large chunk of ceiling came down with a crash, off balancing en route a porcelain bedside lamp which promptly joined the fragments on the floor.

Hardly had I kicked the worst of the ruin beneath the bed when the Deputy Manager stood at the door. He clicked his teeth sadly while surveying the damaged ceiling.

"Ach, things are not what they used to be," he muttered, his eyes totting up the forints to be added to my bill.

His words admirably summed up the Hungary of 1955. In East Germany it had been Vopo's and ticket collectors. But for Hungary the yardstick was undoubtedly hotel bells.

I had arrived in Budapest that warm July morning exactly ten months after my return from Berlin. The set-back in Germany had not been allowed to defeat either Anna or myself and in the spring of 1955 two further glimmers of hope flickered in the darkness. First one and then another republic of fettered Eastern Europe, long denied to Western tourists, opened its well-guarded doors a creaking inch or so to a few favoured travel agencies. The numbers of tourists these Agents were allowed to send was small and tightly controlled, whilst the itinerary of the tours themselves were to a strict pattern. Two of the Agencies concerned were British and the countries from whence the cautious invitations had stemmed were Hungary and Czechoslovakia.

It was Hungary that started it. Immediately I learnt of the tour I applied for participation and was fortunate to get a place as the number of participants was limited to fifteen.

The announcement concerning the proposed Czechtour came later. It was something of an historic occasion and the Czech Government was going to make capital out of it. Somewhat cynically I applied to the obscure Agency in South London whose managing director had been the unsuccessful Communist candidate for Tottenham. The fact that members of his tour were expected to wear red peace-dove badges made me wince as I completed the forms, but this would be a small price to pay for a whole fortnight with Anna. However, the chances of my being granted a visa particularly for a prestige affair like this were infinitely smaller. Grimacing at the prospect of a lost deposit I posted the forms. Nothing ventured nothing gained.

The Hungarian authorities in the meantime could find no reason to deny me entry to their fair land and since this tour ended a full week before the Czech one began I had nothing to lose. The Agency for the Hungarian venture was a well-known West End establishment with no political axes to grind and it was clearly emphasized to those participating that the tour was in the nature of an experiment.

The first day of July found me sitting dejectedly on a pile of someone else's luggage amidst the bustle of Salzburg Station. So far the experiment had gone far from well and we weren't even in Hungary. My legs ached from fifteen hours of standing in a crowded corridor and my eyes stung through lack of sleep. In pessimistic frame of mind I began chaffing myself for wasting good money on an "experimental" holiday that was, for me, more of a reconnaissance than a serious attempt at making contact with Anna. But an examination of the Danube border between Hungary and Slovakia **could** prove interesting. A wet frontier might well have certain advantages over dry ones and, if so, the knowledge would be vital on a future occasion. I intended nothing provocative on this trip. I would be a good solid citizen so that, if the experiment were repeated (as I had no doubt that our sterling currency would ensure it did), I could return.

Since Anna had been unable to reach even East Germany the previous year there seemed little likelihood of her being allowed to visit Hungary now. A dying uncle in both Budapest and Balatonfoldvar had, however, been invented for the occasion and the Czech emigration authorities did not have to know that her reasons for visiting him were more passionate than compassionate. But I held no hopes of seeing her in either place.

My contemplations were interrupted by a clear English voice posing the question "Are you one of us?" I looked up and beheld a mildly handsome man a little older than myself. He wore a blazer, flannels

67

and a neat black moustache. But it was the girl by his side who stole my interest. She was fair and slim, younger than the man and laughter bubbled in her blue eyes.

I replied that Budapest was my destination whereupon the man, turning to the girl, said "At least we've got one of 'em" from which I deduced him to be the tour leader. Ronald and Joan Plant were soon to become very good friends indeed.

Gradually other members of the party, lurking in various corners of the station, were rounded up and later, in a Vienna hotel, a roll call showed us to be all present and correct. I promptly fell in with a trio of bachelors; Fred Bagley, Derek Haskins and a tall argumentative Scot, Tom Dawson. Genteel respectibility was represented by a couple who had come to visit their married daughter living in Budapest. Timidity surprisingly had a pair of champions in two not-so-young spinsters for whom Worthing would have been a more appropriate hunting ground. A sardonic couple from the Midlands came looking for trouble while the clown of the party was undoubtedly "Aunty"; a mixture of Victorian arrogance and endearing charm encased in wrinkled antiquity. All present, yes, but the Hungarian People's Republic was soon to find us anything but correct!

They would have had a preview at Brueck where the Vienna-Budapest express made one of its many stops. Romantic flutterings awoke within the bosoms of the spinsters at the sight of a platoon of semi-stripped Russian soldiers unloading timber in the sidings of this Austrian town. A battery of cameras were aimed at these strange creatures from another world to the indignant growls of a hairy Warrant Officer who slouched up to the carriage side. Mistaking the burning fuse of his displeasure for bleats of affection the coy smiles of the excited spinsters increased, but fortunately the journey was resumed before the great disillusion.

Hegyeshalom was the frontier and, being an Iron Curtain frontier, came a depressingly familiar routine. But it was "Aunty" who brought a moment of high comedy into the proceedings. A particularly distasteful Hungarian thug chose to search beneath the seats and indicated his intention by prodding her knee with the barrel of his sub-machine gun. Rising to her full diminutive height and stabbing the astounded man in the chest she told him in icy tones exactly what she thought of Hungarian manners. The man fled.

As if to pour oil on troubled waters "Olga" appeared on the scene. With admirable forethought and no doubt for varied other reasons the State had arranged for the English party to be met at the border by an efficient representative of *"Ibusz"*, State Travel Organisation, (S.T.O.) whose job, it became apparent, was to ensure its clients saw the "right" things and have as little as possible contact with the "wrong" type of Hungarians. If we had to be watched the four bachelors could find no fault with the choice of representative the State had made for the job and the buxom shapeliness of Anni Turgonyi met our full approval.

Having introduced herself in a language she believed to be English, the glamorous newcomer took over from Ronald Plant. Bursting with national pride she treated the party to an eulogy on the wonders of Budapest. "So what would you like to see first?" she finished in wide-eyed anticipation.

Tom was up to the occasion, "The slave camp please". His voice matched hers. The good lady was non-plussed; the German and French parties she had conducted had never said things like that...

The train jerked forward without warning and "Olga", smiling fixedly, picked herself from Tom's receptive lap. Her nickname was born from that moment though the resourceful Mrs. Turgonyi was no child of the Soviet Union. Her husband, it was reputed, was a star of the Budapest Opera.

At Gyor "Olga" attempted to distract our attention from the poverty apparent in the shoeless populace. Unsuccessful, she fell back on a phrase that was to cling to her throughout the tour. "We are a poor country", she announced with heart-breaking sadness. But my attention was fastened on to something else. The wide ribbon of the Danube had joined the railway; its green banks speckled with flocks of white geese while small herds of cows, watched over by old women, stood lazily around ancient wooden water pumps that had remained unchanged since biblical times. And across the muddy brown water of the river was Slovakia.

Plainly I could see the same fields and houses but they were in a different world; a world in which my Anna lived but a world as remote for me as the forbidden city of Lhasa. As I looked with fascinated eyes I could feel the warm arms around my neck and the wet tears against my cheek. But the tears could have been my own as the mental picture faded into the reality of the fabled Danube. River of Romance they called it. It was probably booby-trapped.

Komaron had a bridge that made me really sit up and take notice. It carried the road into the promised land and a lot of supporting lattice steel-work was apparent beneath. The steel girder flanges looked wide enough to negotiate and were certainly worthy of closer scrutiny. I carried an image of that bridge with its intriguing possibilities with me to Budapest.

The Astoria Hotel had, like the Hungarian capital, seen better days. The big oak panelled rooms, threadbare velvet curtains and intricately carved marble staircase no longer knew the sound of gaiety or beheld the colourful gowns of ladies of the Austro-Hungarian Court and their dashing escorts. Instead they had to make do with dull, earnest workers' delegations from other peoples' democracies. The lift no longer operated, cold water came from taps marked "hot" and, as I had discovered the first night, the bells provided unintended surprises.

The faded glories of Budapest made a sad backdrop for a regime that despised much of what they stood for. But, in spite of the blood red star of Communism that defiled the historic palaces and the concrete memorials to a liberation that wasn't, the spirit of Lajos Kossuth showed through the facade.

Most of the sightseeing was to be carried out by bus for obvious reasons, but *Ibusz* had reckoned without the ideas of a strongly individualistic English group who refused to be regimented. Long before the coach had put in an appearance "Olga's" charges had evaporated into the city. Only once did she catch us for a visit to the Sports Stadium and that was quite enough.

From an English-speaking waiter in the hotel who once lived in Surrey, I learnt of the extent of travel restrictions in the Hungarian Republic and on the third morning played the usual truant with "Olga". The previous evening at the communal dinner I had left her with the impression that I was going on a river trip to view the architectural splendours. At the Nyugari Station half expecting a repetition of the East German ticket farce I was pleasantly surprised to find myself installed in a Komaron - bound train with no more difficulty than is normal when two people converse in tongues utterly meaningless to the other. In a way I had told "Olga" the truth since a certain Danube bridge held, for me, considerable architectural interest.

Three hours later, with the life of the busy town flowing about me, I was gazing at my objective. Its approaches formed the centre of Komaron and on the Czech side of the river their portion of the town, Komarno, was similarly situated. The usual frontier restrictions existed at each end of the bridge. Along the banks of the swiftly-flowing waters were a number of watch-towers, but those on the Hungarian shore were, as far as I could see, unoccupied.

70

I gave closer attention to the underside of the bridge itself. Supported on large concrete buttresses the framework of the structure rested on two huge T-girders slightly arched. The inner lower flanges were wide and low enough beneath the road canopy to support a man. Given a dark night, a pair of rubber shoes...

I should have known better of course, but the permanent record of a photograph would be so useful. Surreptitiously I removed my camera from its case, shielded it with my jacket and with difficulty focused it on the girders. Even railway stations are classed as defence installations in a people's democracy as I well knew. Border bridges are white hot. Coinciding with the click of my shutter came an ear-splitting yell from above. Glancing up I saw a policeman, outrage written all over him, turn and begin pounding along the bridge to cut me off. Hastily I closed the camera and bundled it into my pocket. Nobody else had noticed my action though the shout had aroused considerable attention. People were looking up at the running man not realising that the object of his wrath stood amongst them.

A semi-circular square surrounded the bridge approach from which, like spokes of a wheel, narrow streets radiated into the town. The nearest was just behind me. If I could get into it without being noticed I could successfully lose myself.

Backing slowly, watching my pursuer still running in the opposite direction before he could attain the end of the bridge, I was tempted to turn and flee. Only when the walls of the buildings loomed protectively over me did I turn about and at a fast walk make tracks for the station.

An Englishman in the back streets of Komaron was a comparative rarity and the stares I received from a mainly peasant population kept me moving. But no hue and cry developed and for once in my life a railway station featured as a welcome sanctuary. A traveller of any creed or colour can be tolerated on a station, but had there been a train in that was going anywhere I would have caught it. As it was my last hour in Komaron was spent cringing in the loo.

In thoughtful mood I caught an early afternoon train back to Budapest.

My colleagues were most intrigued by the attention I received from "Olga" at dinner that night. She almost purred with good humour even when the Hungarian sickle and ear of wheat emblem that adorned our table somehow contrived to fall in the soup tureen. Interwoven with the pleasantries, however, came the sharp questions

71

about my day's outing. I was able to give as good as I got, however, for between my return to the capital and dinner I had managed to take in a short river trip.

A coach outing to Eger where a substantial sample of *Egri Bikaver*, or "Bull's Blood", the red wine of the region, made this an accepted outing reasonably worthwhile and a fitting end to the first half of the holiday. But with Balatonfoldvar "Olga" could relax for in this tourist resort sprawling with others, along the shore of the placid shallow waters of Lake Balaton this was the Hungary of the travel agency brochures.

One night towards the end of the second week I found myself trying to dance a tango with "Olga". The evenings were the only time we came to life, after a day's soaking by sun and water. She hugged me to her well proportioned bosom and whispered, "you look sad Christophair. You think of your Anna I theenk". Through the alcoholic haze a red light flashed at me.

I murmured something non-committal.

"She is not so far away, Christophair. There are difficulties; there are always difficulties in these things but I know all will end happily. We are a poor country."

Clumsily steering her away from a table laden with empty glasses I thought I saw what she meant by her fabled phrase.

Later she asked me to take her for a row on the lake. With the fairy lights of Balatonfoldvar sparkling on the waters and the sad airs of gipsy music filling the balmy night she was very ready for me to make love to her. But my desires lay elsewhere and the magic of the night was not for me. Sometimes I think of lost opportunities.

But this first cautious invitation to Western tourists ended on a joyous note. A visit to the Benedictine abbey at Tihany across the lake resulted in an unscheduled visit to a wine-bottling cellar nearby. This developed into a mammoth party involving a high percentage of the Tihany populace when, in tribute to the English visitors, the normal tourist issue of one sample glass of wine went by the board. To the vigorous music of half-a-dozen violins the Balaton Hills were soon ringing to the strains of British and Hungarian national airs as we, in company with our new friends, swept down to the lake with the vague idea of catching the last steamer. Fred and I, having no particular desire to catch it, proceeded to jump in the lake in our underpants from which, as the steamer siren hooted in derision, "Olga" literally dragged us. The cheer that went up from a thousand throats as our state "protector" propelled her two unco-operative and near naked English charges up the gangway will be a legend for years to come.

In spite of this it was a subdued and rather sad "Olga" who took leave of her English party next day at Budapest's West Station.

"See you one day in London," I told her and meant it.

"We are a poor country and there are difficulties, but—," she gave me a dazzling smile, "but one day maybe I come." Her voice faded into the general goodbyes as the train glided out.

Difficulties, always difficulties, I mused slamming shut the compartment door in the surprised face of a prowling Customs Officer.

With a day to spare in Salzburg I made my first port of call the main Post Office on the off-chance that my parents had sent me a letter there rather than risk the erratic postal connections with Hungary. I was rewarded with a missive from my mother. It gave a resume of the local news, a report on the garden, a description of a room of the house she was redecorating and asked how I was enjoying my holiday. And there was a postscript which read: "Oh yes, there is a letter from the Czech Embassy granting you a visa."

CHAPTER 8

Palaver in Prague

A prominent person once said of the British Communist Party: "This alien-controlled organisation is composed of members who, if they are good Communists, are by definition traitors to their own country".

To me, being borne swiftly across Southern Germany in a portion of the Orient Express to which I was becoming familiar, this utterance was being given full emphasis. All around me in the the reserved compartment were members and sympathisers of the British Communist Party, all obediently wearing their little dove badges and all stolidly believing their own preposterous lies simply because it was the party line.

At Victoria station I had felt it expedient to sport my badge but had felt such deep shame (particularly when a porter had sarcastically addressed me as "comrade") that I had hidden my light under a bushel by transferring the thing to my pocket. During the journey I had steadfastly pretended I was nothing to do with my thirty-five "fellow travellers" whose tirades on slave conditions prevalent in the United Kingdom become louder and wilder as the journey proceeded. A particularly loathsome specimen—a gimlet-eyed woman enveloped in a bright orange dress—whose mouth was the loudest of the lot once or twice provoked me into heated denial though fear of being labelled a "reactionary" before the Czech border was behind us forced me for the most part to suffer in silence. As the train drew into Schirnding "blabbermouth" started up again with a forecast on how long the wicked Americans would hold up the train. Since I knew the form at Schirnding and Cheb only too well I forebade to comment since facts would speak for themselves. They did only too clearly but the good lady took it in her stride. She had it all pat. Those American spies; **of course** the progressive Czechs had to take precautions. It was **quite** understandable. Like others of her kind she had a marked dislike of anything American. I could only but admire her colossal self-deception.

On the platform of Cheb station I looked out for my S.N.B. officer. Before he had apoplexy I wanted to show him I had a visa. But he was not in sight. Maybe he only did his stint at Easter. However, there was a reception committee of another sort.

Self-conscious in national costume several girls, not very enthusias-
tically, distributed flowers to the first British tourist since the New
Order. A drizzle was falling and the "Peace" banners hung limp in
the grey afternoon. The thump of a polka, top heavy with off-key
brass, came from a scruffy army band and, to show nothing had changed,
the ring of guards were only a little less conspicuous as they surrounded
the contaminated train.

My Commie compatriots had a field day. Bleating treason they
treated the curious Czech to a catalogue of the horrors of life in
Britain most of which had come straight out of the pages of Charles
Dickens. "Blabbermouth" held court as she attempted to explain to
a perplexed audience how pleased she was to breathe the free, untainted
air of the New Czechoslovakia. Where I could I went round quietly
making amends but noticed one of the three tour conductors giving
me a shrewd look. I would have to stay at heel a little longer.

The tour was based upon Marianske Lazne, or Marienbad. A highly
organised programme of events, including attendance at a Trade
Union meeting and a radio interview, was crammed into the schedule
to keep any non-believers from getting the wrong idea. I was to meet
Anna at Marienbad just over an hour away. That, for me, was the
beginning and end of my programme. The rest was purely incidental.

The train pulled out of Cheb an hour and a quarter late and seemed
in no way inclined to make up for lost time. It dawdled serenely
through the dark satanic pinewoods of the Bohmerwald—the long
straight ranks of trees like frozen sentinels. Occasionally the ranks
were broken where rock-strewn streams and waterfalls forced their
way through the eternal parade and Carlsbad itself injected a grey
Victorian elegance into the timber parade-ground.

Looking at the sullen splendour of the scene my eyes saw only Anna.
Within forty minutes I would be with this strange and wonderful
girl who had waited so patiently those hopeless years. Within forty
minutes we would be out of the shadow into the light. I shook my
head in disbelief but it was no dream. My heart thudded violently.
With fourteen endless days all our own we would sweep aside the
ministerial barriers a truculent Interior Ministry department had set
up. Together we could conquer the world. But what if they had not
let her come to Marienbad? Could they stop her from coming to a
town in an unrestricted zone? I knew damn well they could as the
doubts and the optimism see-sawed in my mind. The train began to
brake at the outer suburbs of the spa and the answers to my hopes
and fears were at hand.

Beating the orange-sheathed ambassadress to the open window by a short head I scrutinised the station approaches as if my life depended upon it. A goods train rattled by in the opposite direction and I cursed inwardly as my view flickered like a home movie. With the last wagon out of the way we passed into the shadow of the station roof and a sea of faces stared straight back at me. The noise of another band came to my ears and a display of bunting warned of a second reception committee.

The sea diffused into a blur of curious eyes as I wildly searched for the one face that mattered. Even when the train stopped I went on staring out oblivious of the grins and jocular remarks I was collecting. Last out of the coach I walked, half in a daze, up the gap in the crowd that cleared for me. Someone pushed a bunch of flowers into my hand. I looked quickly at the donor but saw only a stranger. Kind, friendly, simple faces pressed around me asking questions about a world that was locked out of their lives. I tried to smile back but my mind fought again with a deepening dread. Would I be able to leave the group and make my way to Anna's home? The likelihood was slim indeed. An authority that could impose restrictions on her movements was equally capable of restricting mine. Maybe she was at the hotel. I had told her it was the Zapotocky. Yes, she could be there. Desperately I clutched at straws and moved faster towards the exit.

Suddenly she stood before me. The tears were unchecked in her turquoise eyes and her mouth was an 'O' of wonderment. I stopped abruptly and looked at her as if she was the last person on earth I expected to see. She began smiling through the tears and the spell was broken. Clasped in my arms her warm mouth found my own and in the middle of a crowd of several hundred onlookers we found the solace usually reserved for the more intimate of occasions.

The audience was delighted and roared their approval showering us with flowers. Undoubtedly we had given them a demonstration of Anglo-Czech solidarity that no political or labour delegation could ever hope to achieve. One of the tour organisers returned to see what the fuss was about and stood perplexed, slightly disapproving, as we finished our own private welcome. Apparently we were holding up an official speech, so hand in hand, wildly content, we passed into the station booking hall.

Hemmed in by the crowds on all sides we looked into each other's eyes revelling in the joy of reunion while all the while the local dignitaries waffled on about peaceful co-existence. Anna and I could not have agreed more! Neither of us heard the translation as we clung to each other as if reassuring ourselves that this was not just another dream.

As we took our seats in the crowded bus Anna produced a bunch of carnations somewhat wilted from long handling within a small hot fist.

"I almost forgot these," she said laughing and thrust the flowers at me.

"I'll look a like walking garden," I replied and then realised we had spoken our first words together for two long years.

More crowds surrounded the imposing portals of the Zapotocky Hotel and yet another band played boisterously beneath a slogan-laden banner. But inside, in the cold stone interior, peace held full sway and for the first time in our lives we experienced the exhilaration of being alone with each other.

Dinner in the pillared dining room was an excuse for more speeches but even a long recitation by the Mayor of Marienbad became an ordeal that, with Anna by my side, was pleasant enough.

Only in the late evening were we able to escape from the maddening receptions, the inane remarks of my countrymen and the inquisitive stares of the Czechs, to go out into the ill-lit streets of the town and become just another couple to haunt the shadows. And, as is the right of every lover in a hundred lands, to experience the balm of serene happiness.

The running of the tour bore a marked resemblance to its Hungarian counterpart, but there were certain differences, not the least of which was the eager docility of the larger group on the Czech tour. In Budapest little notice had been taken of the programme laid down by *Ibusz* but, in Marienbad, the daily trips fixed by *Cedok* were compulsory and attended without question. *Cedok*, the state travel organisation of Czechoslovakia, again took over from the British tour leader whilst on Czech territory and attached four "interpreters" to the group. The fact that only two of them spoke English provoked no comment, even though their real purpose was obvious from the start. Throughout the fortnight the tour was based upon Marienbad and to stomach the heavy programme of industrial and cultural visits heavily spiced with a political flavour one had to be either a dedicated Communist or blessed with a wry sense of humour. Though some of the visits were not without interest the very nature of them was alien to the Englishman's traditional idea of holidaymaking and the "off-duty" evenings in the Marienbad hall of culture, in which members were encouraged to fraternise with their comrades of other Eastern European groups, were positively abhorrent.

Into this maelstrom of industrial and political glorification and organised spontaneity Anna and I were flung on the wave of circumstances. Hardly did we leave one another's side and Anna became an accepted member of the group accompanying me on the scheduled excursions and eating with me in the hotel. Invariably we remained in the background though our situation gradually became the object of sympathetic interest.

On the fourth day the coach took us to Prague and the opportunity for which Anna and I had been waiting. One of the most beautiful cities in the world it lay under a sun-tinted, cloud-filled sky, inviting exploration. But the picture postcard Hradcany Castle and Cathedral of St. Vitus casting their eternal gaze upon the lesser spires and turrets of the old town were not for us. Nor were the narrow streets and alleys nestling in the shadows of history. Instead we had sterner business to transact.

Slipping quietly away from the group as they gazed obediently at the carvings in Jan Hus' Bethlehem Chapel, Anna and I made our way across the ancient Charles Bridge spanning the weir-divided waters of the Vltava River and through the old town to the block of stone buildings that housed the British Embassy. Here we would begin the skirmish to prize loose the bureaucratic hold a government had on one of its citizen victims.

Leaving Anna at a nearby cafe I entered the gates with its polish-worn brass plate; a little bit of England in a foreign field. The blue-uniformed policeman saluted politely recognising me as English and I knew that his duties included taking the names of Czech subjects bold enough to do likewise. Already Anna had tasted the acid fruits of such action and the resulting attentions of the Security Police.

Within the massive walls the Englishman's castle became an exaggeration of the English way of life, an implied token of displeasure at the way the rest of the world lives. From a battered leather arm-chair the pipe-smoking Consul, fondling an old school cravat, listened to my tale of woe and then, with me, discussed ways and means of persuading a Communist Government to relinquish one of its captives.

It was a depressing conversation. Already Anna's first application to marry a foreigner and, by implication, to emigrate, had been rejected and the Consul himself had, within the limits imposed by diplomatic procedure, taken up the matter with the Czech authorities. Results had been meagre indeed and the only success that could be claimed was the negative one of a reply to the third prompting saying ''No''!

Before we parted the Consul showed interest in the composition of my fellow "holidaymakers" and asked if he could join, incognito, the radio recording session arranged for that night in a Trade Union hotel he still insisted upon calling the "Imperial". What seemed to interest him particularly was the fact that the British-born wives of Czechs, living in Prague, had been invited to attend and, en masse, dispute the lies of a capitalistic press ignorant enough to doubt their well-being in the Czechoslovak People's Paradise. I couldn't but agree to his request and to his view that, if nothing else, it would be good for a giggle.

The central headquarters of the Ministry of the Interior seemed fair game for the next, and, this time, combined onslaught by Anna and myself. Girding our loins we stormed the thick plate-glass doors. The advance lost momentum a little as we came upon a squad of S.N.B. men bristling with rapid-fire artillery looking like something Fidel Castro left behind in the Cuban jungles.

"We've come to the wrong place," I said executing a swift wheelabout. "This is the Ministry of War."

"They're all like this," whispered Anna calmly and checked my withdrawal.

In some perplexity I gazed at the guardians of security, my mind attempting to adjust itself from the expected vision of Victorian dignity observed on the occasional visits I had paid to London ministries.

To a weasel-faced corporal with a hedgehog for a chin I gave up my passport for examination and Anna her miniature encyclopedia of an identity card. Both comprised substantial reading matter and the man was a slow reader.

"We want the Emigration Department," Anna stated simply.

The corporal continued his reading.

"Why?" he asked suddenly.

Anna gave him the general idea.

This produced one grunt and two forms. The grunt was gratis but the form demanded, in a manner slightly less brusque than voiced by Che Quevara, the reasons for the pleasure of our company.

Anna proceeded to write out the general idea.

Armed with our life histories but minus passports and identity cards, the advance continued up a flight of stairs. On a landing a mere civilian guarded a desk. He looked at us enquiringly.

"The Emigration Department, please," said Anna.

The man read the forms with deliberation. To prove his superiority over the licentious soldiery he asked primly: "Whom do you wish to see?"

"The Minister", Anna's reply was almost a challenge.

The official gazed at her through his spectacles, removed them and tried again. Satisfied that he was seeing what he thought he saw he put them back.

"The Minister," he repeated, as if also in doubt of his hearing. "Have you an appointment?"

"No, but we want to make one."

The official felt himself on safer ground. "You must write an application for an interview."

Anna was not impressed. "Why cannot we apply here and now?" she asked and before the wretched man could dream up an answer let go a verbal broadside. Up to this moment I had been able to follow the gist of the exchange but gave up as the angry flow of Czech poured over the wilting clerk.

With the last drip I got in a question. "What was all that about?"

"I told him you were here only for ten days," she said. I marvelled at a woman's ability to say so much about so little.

The little clerk capitulated. For one "so dressed in a brief authority" he had no hope against an aroused Anna. **And** with a rare specimen of Englishman in tow. Though his rulers hurled a veneer of insults at Britain his fellow Czechs undeniably held solid respect for those Anglo-Saxons. The man spoke into a telephone.

"The Minister's Secretary will see you," he whispered as if awed by what he had done. "But you will have to wait a few minutes."

The "few minutes" totalled forty before a suave young man appeared. Anna and I rose expectantly from the hard chairs.

"Sorry you've been kept waiting", the man apologised in English. An apology **and** in my own language. We must be getting somewhere I thought. The suave young man went on to explain that the secretary would see us that afternoon in the other building. He gave Anna the details. Withdrawing we collected our identity documents from the guerilla force in the vestibule.

The "other building" was in the Dejvice district. It was an ugly concrete-faced structure plentifully endowed with red stars and blue slogans. The colourful decor did nothing to improve it.

I am positive that the squad of S.N.B. men that received us were the same as those of the previous encounter. Either that or they all had brothers. I thought I knew what it was like to be a victim of one of those old Keystone Cop movies. Stepping warily in case of hidden manholes I followed Anna to Corporal "Che's" relation.

It started again. "We wish to see the Minister's secretary," said Anna.

"Che II" opened his mouth to say "Why?" but was checked by Anna's hurried: "We have an appointment."

Instead he said "Passports."

Anna's identity card he passed over as beneath contempt but made a great show of examining my passport. He beamed at the visas of the Peoples' Democracies, tolerated those of the "neutral" states and positively snarled at the lone eagle of the United States. Again we were presented with two forms.

For a change I completed mine in English and following a telephone call for instructions we were directed to the first floor, Room 15.

The door said 'knock and wait' or words to that effect. We did. Nothing happened. A girl came out of number fourteen and said that it was number sixteen we wanted. I began to look for manholes again. Sixteen said knock and enter.

A girl at a typewriter smiled at us. "The Minister's Secretary will see you now," she vouchsafed and indicated an inner office.

The mild, middle-aged character to whom we presented ourselves did not inspire confidence. Having shaken hands and acquainted himself with the facts from a massive dossier he relapsed into a long monologue which was half apology half explanation for the delay and trouble the department was causing us. It was as good a bit of Communist clap-trap as I have heard and, in a long devious way, meant precisely nothing. Looking down from the wall was the Lord and Master, the Minister, Josef Barak, who surely would have approved of his minion's recital. We were ushered out half satisfied that something was being done and it was only as we compared notes afterwards that we saw how easily we had been taken for a ride.

It was late afternoon before we got to the ex- "Imperial" hotel but still in time for the Radio Prague recording session. The cause of its delay appeared to be the non-arrival of the British-born wives and their important verbal "proof" of idyllic conditions within the Czechoslovak State.

Sitting aloof from the group was the British Consul. He showed obvious delight at our arrival since he was fast becoming the object of suspicious glances from all and sundry. He was also beginning to wonder if his presence was having anything to do with the consciences of the reticent wives!

Because the programme was due to be broadcast the following day proceedings were not delayed further and began with the announcer asking various members of the group for their impressions which were dutifully given. I noticed he picked only on the steadfastly "reliable" members avoiding like the plague me and one or two "waverers". Half-way through these preliminaries a panting wife appeared on the scene much to the relief of the producer.

"So sorry I'm late," she wheezed loudly between gasps for breath. "Got stuck in one of those bloody meat queues the other end of town." The recording engineer made frantic efforts to erase several inches of tape. Someone sniggered in the audience.

The lone wife was then subjected to a series of mild questions put to her by the chosen few of the group but to my acute disappointment she failed to live up to her promising start. I never even attempted a spontaneous question since it was certain to be of the "unconstructive" type and therefore would never attain the ether.

At the end of the performance the group were quickly herded on to the waiting coach for the drive back to Marienbad. Our Czech "interpreters" were already in a bad mood owing to the upsetting of the timetable and their tempers were not improved when, following a check, it was discovered that one of their doves was missing. The errant bird was me and since Anna and I had unfinished business in Prague we intended to remain another day. Quite a violent little scene was enacted in the hotel foyer when we announced our decision and I derived great pleasure from my first open revolt.

"I shall come back to Marienbad in due course," I finished. I wasn't even going to tell them that it would probably be tomorrow.

"But you can't stay on your own," the tour leader chimed in with growing concern.

"Why not?" Anna's voice lashed back.

"It's strictly forbidden," came the reply which was the stock Communist answer to anything that was not a stock question.

Anna was not to be deterred. "Why should a night in Prague be forbidden?"

The interpreter was becoming impatient. "For you, no, but Mr. Portway is a foreigner and he is registered at Marienbad. If he remains here he will be arrested."

"But he will register here in the hotel tonight."

A look of vast relief crossed the interpreter's face.

"Oh, you're not staying at a private house then?"

"No, we shall book rooms at this hotel."

The interpreter, mollified, returned to the coach content that he had not been party to the crime of allowing an Englishman to spend the night under a private Czech roof. Only the leader seemed doubtful about loosing one of his doves. Or maybe because he was beginning to realise that he had a pigeon in the flock.

With a night alone together in a city of repression, we tried to find laughter. We drank inferior vermouth at an inferior night club and danced on a crowded floor to a second-rate orchestra. But though content to be in each other's company we found no laughter. And the lone man who stood near our table and followed us to our hotel in the early hours of the morning seemed to find nothing to laugh at either.

The beds were hard and lumpy and the breakfast of ersatz coffee offered little consolation. But the sun was shining again in a watery sky. Paying a small fortune for the beds and coffee we left the hotel. The sun was free even in Czechoslovakia.

Our next task was a more ambitious one. To start at the bottom and work up the ladder is an unoriginal and tedious method of getting anywhere. Better, surely, to start at the top. Convinced of the soundness of our reasoning we set out to call on the President of the Republic.

Many stories were rife concerning President Antonin Zapotocky. Few were complimentary, though it was said that he played the accordion well when drunk. I liked accordion music so at least we had one thing in common.

As all Presidents should, Comrade Zapotocky lived in a castle. His was the Castle of Hradcany and a number 23 tram passed the door. This mode of vehicle had to pass for a coach and horses in a People's Democracy, and anyway, with an exchange rate of twenty crowns to the pound, I would have clicked for the tram anyway. The sentries were a disappointment, too. No scarlet warriors parading up and down. Instead a handful of peasant soldiers with the usual hardware lounged around the main gate. We walked straight through ignoring their presence. In turn the soldiers ignored ours.

No quaint notice in the cobbled courtyard read "To the President" but there was one indicating an office. It only sold postcards but we decided it would do for a start.

Anna made her request in Czech and got an old-fashioned look. An obliging S.N.B. man sauntered up to supply the necessary information and we were on our way.

"Who did you ask for?" I queried, "the King of the castle?"

Anna gave me a stony glance. "The Presidential Office," she said.

"How do we know his Lordship's at home?"

"Because the man told me."

Marvelling again at the determination and composure of the woman I had chosen for a wife we clattered like a small regiment of cavalry over a series of courtyards, down echoing stone corridors and up granite steps. We came to a door. On it was a notice which read "Presidential Office. Appointments only".

The S.N.B. man standing in front of it wore a crease in his trousers and his artillery was a diminutive and refined little pistol. Also he had shaved. Obviously we were nearing the upper reaches of the hierarchy.

Anna spoke to him and the man politely opened the door for us. But Mr. Zapotocky was not waiting, enthroned, within to receive us. Only a mousy little man in a high-backed chair. Again Anna explained our mission.

"Come back again this afternoon," she was told. "Two till four is the time for applying for presidential interviews."

The clock on the wall said five to twelve.

Anna explained that I was an English visitor as if she was saying "Abracadabra."

The mousy man did indeed show a spark of interest and retreated into an inner office. I put my tongue out at a marble bust of Karl Marx. In silent expectancy we waited.

The man reappeared. "The President's Secretary will see you," he announced and ushered us into the inner sanctum.

We entered a room of almost palatial quality. A Persian carpet hid the floor and gentle illumination came from exquisite cut-glass chandeliers. A young man in a dark suit rose from behind a giant mahogany desk.

84

Anna spoke her piece.

The secretary was sympathetic. He wrote copious notes on a piece of paper. He even called for a stenographer who wrote some more, But he couldn't produce a president, not even a small one. No, nobody could actually **see** the President; not just like that. But he would be made personally aware of the case. The President was a very busy man indeed. Affairs of state, you know. I strained my ears for accordion music.

But he could promise one thing. Anna could make another marriage application and he himself would see that the President gave it personal consideration. And the President, as all Czechoslovakia knew so well, was a kind and considerate man.

Satisfied that his benign words had spread joy and gratitude the secretary retreated behind the desk. Maybe he even believed them himself.

The stone corridors re-echoed to our footfalls as we retraced our steps but the echoes were less sprightly. The busiest people around here I thought were secretaries acting as buffers for their ministers. I glared ferociously at a leather-jacketed youth trying not to look like a security man.

Because it was a stone unturned we returned in the afternoon. The outer office was full of people craving interviews with a President they would never see. We gave it up.

In the evening we returned to Marienbad, two sadder but wiser people. Perhaps no wiser for Anna had started out with no expectations and I, to be honest, only needed the evidence of my own eyes and ears. The sum total of our accomplishments had been permission for Anna to make another marriage application. If that failed we were left with the only alternative action open to us. The Elbe below Bad Schandau, the rolling hills near Horni Dvoriste, a bridge at Komaron; all pointed a way. But another barrier loomed, more indistinct and evil even than barbed wire and mines. Its name was retribution. Like the ostrich I pretended it wasn't there. As our train sped through the parched Bohemian countryside I learnt the truth, the bitter truth, that our escape would open an account with the state. And Anna's aged parents and her two sisters would remain behind to pay the bill.

Darkness enveloped us as the train plunged into a tunnel. Our hands met and clasped tightly. Faith was our only friend.

CHAPTER 9

Czechmate

Only the weather did its best to shatter the illusion of carefree abandon for the rest of the holiday. Flinging ourselves into the assorted activities of the group, we found something akin to happiness with only the relentless approach of the holiday's end to give the silver cloud a grey lining. But there was nothing silvery about the clouds above; unceasingly they belched water on to sodden ground below. That it curtailed some of the activities could be counted as a blessing though, as a rainy day at the seaside, the gloom could but only increase our own.

It rained each time we visited the nearby "Riviera" swimming pool that had a hard time living up to its name. It rained at Baron Skoda's castle near Pilsen, drenching his successors, the elite of the country's workers to whom a considerate state had given the turreted mansion as a holiday centre, and it rained for the football match between members of the tour and "Marienbad United" which resulted in a resounding defeat for Great Britain. Only once did the sun succeed in bursting through the grey curtain and upon this precious afternoon did Anna and I stroll up into the pine-clad hills and sit together amongst the steaming corn stooks. High above the villas of Marienbad we looked out across the quiet valleys of the Tepelske Vrchy while the birds sang in the trees around us. And here in our secret eyrie we spoke of plans for the future and, in each other's arms, found solace for the present.

Mostly, however, we found it prudent to remain with the group for the rest of the tour—a prudence encouraged by the unsecretive presence of the secret police who rarely left us to our own devices. They were always following in our wake, listening and watching. Even the members of the group were better company than these silent footpads and I was gratified to note the increasing sympathy and indignation that our plight was producing within the English breasts. Our "interpreters" were quick to notice the change in attitude of their British guests and realised that the small canker was having an effect far more damaging than its worth. They would never understand that, for the average simple-minded Englishman, politics must take a back seat when the well-being of dogs, cats and lovers is at stake.

With minds blinkered by protest in terms of demonstrations, delegations and petitions several members turned upon their "protectors" and threatened to march upon some vague authority existing mainly in their imagination. It all petered out like a damp squib, of course, but this small token resistance gave Anna and myself considerable comfort.

In the meantime the programme ground on. The tour of the lager brewery of Pilsner Urquell was perhaps the most universally enjoyed. Walking down the long, dank tunnels that ran beneath the city I was amazed at the quantity of barrelled lager stored in enormous vats that squatted like bloated coffins in caverns hewn from solid rock. Pilsen was literally aground on a subterranean ocean of beer! Sobering thought or not, the amount of lager the party managed to sink at the luncheon given by the directors afterwards was anything but sobering. The speeches sent most of us to sleep but I do recollect one hoary classic about the wise ones in the West, the philosophers and the sociologists, who accept that war is a necessary evil. It is needed, they said, to reduce the population, to balance the economy and so on.

The speaker, a lean-faced apostle of Lenin, then really got into his stride. In the old days the British said: "We must expand and colonise; build up an Empire upon which the sun never sets. If the ignorant natives resist, shoot them down".

Hitler yelled: "*Lebensraum*! We want more living space. Let us push back the frontiers which are hemming us in. If the Czechs and Poles resist, shoot them down".

How the simile fitted the hated United States I was not to know since at that point in the discourse I fell asleep in company with most of my compatriots and fellow Empire builders. But I am sure he made a good job of it for I was awakened by loud and prolonged clapping.

I could well have added a simile myself about a certain country in the East whose territorial ambitions and methods of conquest embraced the lot. Wasn't it the peace-loving U.S.S.R. who proclaimed: "East is East and West is West, and never the twain shall meet or mix. The Westerners must keep out, and should any dare to intrude we will shoot them down?" And to this end they constructed a monstrous fabrication of iron and steel, of guns and tanks, splitting Europe in two and leaving families crying pitifully for friends, relatives and loved ones wrenched apart. Wasn't this just one result of the great empire-building of Mother Russia? I fostered an idea it was but maybe it was just the beer...

The pilgrimage to Lidice was a far less jovial affair. Having seen the war-destroyed village I found its transformation into a Communist shrine particularly nauseating. Spurning the visitors book Anna and I strolled down the lines of "Peace" roses donated by such militant-sounding left-wing organisations as "The Partisans of Peace" of many European countries. The blooms were wilting and washed out by an overdose of rain, though maybe this was not the only reason they hung their heads in shame.

On the thirteenth, and last, day of the tour it stopped raining. This alone was an event, but in addition, the sun came out in an aggressive, authoritative manner clearly intimating it was there to stay. Playing truant from a scheduled inspection of a glass factory Anna and I spent the day roaming in the peaceful seclusion of the forests. The thought of the inevitable parting on the morrow weighed heavily upon us as we strolled hand in hand along a winding path that followed a swollen stream. The damp undergrowth gave up a faint phosphorescent mist that accentuated the rays of the morning sun poking straight fingers through the trees. The silence was broken by the steady dripping of water-laden branches and an impatient gurgling of the miniature torrent.

With a glow in her cheeks and a wisp of hair falling unbidden across her brow, Anna made an appealing picture. It was one I resolved to carry with me in the lonely days that lay ahead. The ache in my heart became all but unbearable so that I dared not speak. As a shaft of sunlight fell momentarily to her face I saw that she was crying. The skewer of my pain gave another twist but there came a grain of consolation with the thought that another heart besides mine was in torment. Neither of us spoke a word for an eternity and, in a tiny grove of birch trees, we crept for comfort into each other's arms and, still unspeaking, into each other's hearts.

I left the next day on the midday train. In the morning Anna had helped me pack and together we had tried to create the illusion that her foreign marriage and exit permits were just around the corner. The likely number and deviousness of the corners we kept to ourselves as we did any further discussion on the subject of the last resort. Whilst there was an avenue still open to us to take the legal course it was our plain duty to travel it in spite of the pain of continued waiting. To discuss alternatives was tantamount to arguing as to which of us was to sign someone else's death warrant. There was a ray of hope too in the fact that, like Hungary, having been allowed to visit Czechoslovakia there seemed no reason for my being not able to do so again.

My brain was a turmoil as the train drew out of Marienbad station and it helped to steel my heart at the last sight of the lonely figure struggling to hold back her tears. Anna receded from view in the blur of my own tears as I came as near as an Englishman can to crying. My travelling companion was none other than Herbert Lom, the Czech-born film star, and for those poignant moments I like to think I was as good an actor as he.

But while we exchanged polite small-talk it was perhaps fortunate for both his and my peace of mind that I was unaware of the Czech authorities' decision, already in the pipeline, to reject Anna's second application and, at the same time, deny me further entry into Czechoslovakia.

CHAPTER 10

Hawks and Doves

The leaves on the old wych elm had turned brown and were falling at the annual command of autumn when I received the news. The great tree at the bottom of the garden in my home at Great Maplestead had been a secret source of pleasure to me ever since childhood, and for many years I had watched the brown carpet spread across the lawn at the end of summer and, with the advent of spring, the tender new shoots of the honeysuckle that clung to the gnarled trunk. This autumn, however, the falling leaves were but a cruel mockery of the tears I longed to shed.

It was Anna herself who first told me of the further refusal of the Czechoslovak Ministry of the Interior to allow her to marry me. It was confirmed by the British Embassy in Prague and finally by the Czechoslovak Embassy in London who added, for good measure, that I was not to visit their country again under any pretext. All this, in any language, spelt a very definite "No". It was, however, not an answer I was prepared to accept. Hiding my grief I sprang into action with my pen on the assumption that it was mightier than the sword. But I kept my sword well oiled all the same.

During the months that followed I made contact with a host as varied as the colours of a rainbow. I wrote to the Foreign Minister, the Home Secretary, the Minister of State for Foreign Affairs and a prominent Socialist M.P. who had become a specialist in the reunion of families separated by the gulf of extremist politics. I had interviews with officials of the Home and Foreign Office and officers of the Intelligence Departments of the War Office (later to become Ministry of Defence). I requested intervention from the Chairman of the Council of Ministers of the U.S.S.R., Mr. N. A. Bulganin and the Secretary of the Presidium of the Supreme Soviet of the U.S.S.R., Mr. N. S. Krushchev, who had succeeded Stalin. Likewise I applied to the Secretary General of the United Nations Organisation, Mr. Hammarskjold, together with the Director of the United Nations' Division of Human Rights, to do likewise. I asked advice of writers, of Czech refugees, of European refugee organisations, of foreign Embassies, of the Press, of anyone who might be able to shed, wittingly or unwittingly, any light on a subject that lay in the shadow of the unknown. I asked friend and foe alike in an effort to plumb the depths of human beastliness.

Though I stirred the pot of trouble with a steam shovel results at first were meagre. The Foreign Office was aloof and not encouraging. The Embassies remained most diplomatically silent. No joy could be extracted from the two Soviet leaders on the occasion of their State visit to Britain in 1956 though the Foreign Secretary had indeed drawn their attention to the case. The fact that my own M.P. and near-neighbour Mr. (later Lord) R. A. Butler had become Home Secretary was a lucky break though his Ministry was hardly one in a position to help at this stage. He could and did, however—with constant respectful proddings from me—stir the stumps of those who were. Only the War Office, and particularly the silent ones of M.I.5*, became abruptly activated though, alas, not on my account. Being an officer of the Territorial Army I had, overnight, become a "security risk" and, as such, became subject to their attentions. My strange activities in Austria and, more recently, in Czechoslovakia, had come to their notice and I was "on the mat" for polite questioning. But try as I did I could get nothing out of them in return.

A ponderous form of assistance did, however, materialise from the United Nations Organisation, who were persuaded to bring their verbal guns to bear against the Czechoslovak Government at a meeting of the Human Rights Division in New York. But since the object of their censure cared not a fig for the United Nations nothing resulted beyond a sharp reprimand for meddling in its internal affairs. I was desperately grateful for their intervention even if ineffective but I knew that my case had become just another to add to the thousands of minor international problems that remained unsolved.

It was the Honourable Member for Eton and Slough who pulled the biggest—indeed the only—plum out of the bag. I think I can claim the privilege of sharing the friendship of Fenner Brockway (later Lord Brockway), a man whose integrity, understanding and untiring championship of the rights of man put me amongst a great host of similar claimants across the world. But when I first asked for his help I neither knew him or was a member of his flock.

In the second part of his autobiography† Fenner Brockway writes: "He (Christopher Portway) lived in Mr. R. A. Butler's constituency but I was moved by his story and Mr. Butler said he would be glad if I would help because, as a Minister, he could not intervene with a foreign Government. When I went to see the Czech Ambassador I

*The former Military Intelligence branch of the Ministry of Defence. Also M.I.2, Counter Intelligence, were involved.

†"Outside the Right" (George Allen & Unwin Ltd. 1963).

had a shock. He handed me a book and remarked with a wry smile: "Your friend seems to have a flair for Czech girls". The book was of course my own and since, for very good reasons, the last three chapters were decidedly anti-Communist it was now going to be an added cross for me to bear. Fenner Brockway continues: "I was flummoxed. Not for a moment did I believe that the Czechs would put themselves out to help the young man in view of his violently anti-Communist book". It says much for this great socialist warrior and his faith in me that he managed to recover from the shock and take up the cudgels on my behalf.

On his next visit to the Ambassador's comfortable residence in Hampstead Fenner Brockway took me with him. His Excellency Mr. Jiri Hajek had been delayed at the Embassy we were told by a factotum, who looked to me suspiciously like that token of capitalism, a butler, but would we wait. By the time Mr. Hajek put in an appearance we had drunk a considerable quantity of his best slivovice between us. The interview was friendly and, I think, sincere and even though it was with a senior diplomat of the "enemy camp", I felt that in the Czech Ambassador I had, if not a friend, a family man in whose heart the flame of humanity was not dead.*

As well as skirmishing with its representative in London Fenner Brockway was all set to carry the crusade right into the lap of the Czechoslovak Government in Prague. From this he was dissuaded by the Ambassador who thought he could manage the introductionary work better himself on the next routine visit he made to his capital.

I was made aware of these preliminary negotiations and, though the knowledge that somebody was doing something was comforting, my hopes were tinged with cynicism. Quietly I continued to investigate the less orthodox means of gaining the same ends. Among the cosmopolitan population of London I ran to earth many Czechs, Hungarians and East Germans who had "emigrated westwards". Many of these contacts had every reason to remain silent but, piece by piece, I added to my store of knowledge.

In the meantime letters from Anna reached me at infrequent intervals. Many got "lost" but those that survived the censor's eye and the tenuous postal link were cheerful letters, full of optimism and confidence, but in some I detected a note of despair and, occasionally, fear. And on these occasions a cold hand touched my heart, for I knew the reason for that fear...

---

*The fact that, many years later, Jiri Hajek became his country's Foreign Minister of a very much more liberal-minded regime was fitting confirmation of this opinion.

Anna was picking cherries in the garden of her home when they came for her. A hard-faced youth and a girl appeared at the foot of the ladder. They waited in silence.

Halfway up the ladder Anna turned and looked down at the couple.

"You want some cherries," she enquired gaily. People often came to the house for cherries.

The man did not return her smile.

"It is you we want," he spoke quietly, and in an icy undertone went on: "We are from the *Statni Bezpecnost*. You must come with us."

Anna's heart missed a beat. Frequently she had experienced being followed by the S.T.B., or Secret Police, and once they had clumsily accosted her in a train, but never had they actually come for her. But she had known it was only a matter of time.

"May I get my coat?" she asked, descending the ladder.

The S.T.B. man hesitated. "Yes, but tell your mother we are from the Labour Office."

Hurrying into the house, Anna found her mother preparing the midday meal.

"The S.T.B. want me," she explained simply, reaching for her coat from the hall stand. She saw no reason to lie to her own mother to oblige a man ashamed of his trade. As she left Anna had a fleeting vision of a deathly pallor cross the care-worn face.

At the front door she was joined by the sinister couple and by her elder sister who had returned home from work.

"Where are you going?" the latter asked brightly.

Anna looked at the man challenging him to do his own dirty work, but he said nothing. "I don't know," she vouchsafed avoiding her sister's perplexed stare.

A small cream saloon stood a couple of blocks away in a side street. A man in a shabby suit sat at the wheel. Anna was ushered into the back and wedged between the girl and the S.T.B. man. Executing a tight turn in the empty road the driver made for the centre of the town.

On the journey the man spoke only once.

"Why didn't you do as you were told and say we were from the Labour office?" he demanded. It was Anna's turn to remain silent.

The car bumped over the railway crossing and they drew up at police headquarters. In a back room reserved for such purposes Anna was interrogated for three and a half hours. She had nothing to hide but by the time they had finished she was trembling all over. They gave her no dinner and she had to walk home.

Anna was lucky on that occasion. At least she was able to go home. But it was only a matter of time before it would be a one-way excursion. And the sands were fast running out...

Came the summer of 1956. The fear that Anna nursed in her heart had spread to my own. It was fear now that guided my subsequent actions. An early return to Czechoslovakia by either legal means or "fog channel" seemed imperative. It was no good awaiting the well-meaning deliberations of a member of parliament and a diplomat. Time had become another enemy.

As expected a whole string of travel agents throughout the country had "discovered" Czechoslovakia, prompted no doubt by an advantageous rate of exchange, newly introduced. Again the tours were heavily controlled by the Czech travel organisation though the political sting had been taken out of the tail. To keep the Czech consul in London awake I applied to participate in most of them and, had he been less attentive, I would have had to be in Prague, Karlsbad and the Tatra Mountains all at the same time. This welcome problem however did not arise as, one by one, the mystified agents were forced to cancel my booking.

Individual visits, group tours. Both were now denied to me. The London Consulate had got me well and truly taped. The London Consulate, yes. But what about others? And by choosing to visit a country lying north, east or south of Czechoslovakia, could this provide reason for requiring a transit visa? These were less difficult to acquire since their validity was only forty-eight hours. Long enough for my purpose if I could only find a Consul in Europe who didn't know me and I could make out a case strong enough for him to grant one. The case rested, it seemed, upon possession of a visa or proof of sojourn in the neighbouring country of destination.

A study of the map of Europe straightaway eliminated the west to east line of transit for neither the Soviet Union nor Poland were countries to encourage lone visitors or even transitees. This effectively knocked out the Czech consuls of Paris and the capitals of Central and West Europe.

In the south there lay Austria and Hungary. But the Vienna Consulate had already made my acquaintance and consulates, like the secret police, had notoriously long memories. Their man in Budapest had no reason to know me but his line of reasoning was epitomised by the naive request that I obtain the Czech visa first!

Berlin to the north held possibilities but the consulate there had a year less than his colleague in Vienna to forget me. Thus all that remained were the four little nigger boys in the north, the capitals of Scandinavia. Of these Copenhagen and Oslo, geographically, were unlikely candidates since to reach Austria, the obvious goal in the south, there was no real need to pass over Czechoslovak territory at all. But the capitals of Sweden and Finland ... With my head a whirl of airline flight routes and international railway networks I made my plans. Go north, young man.

About the middle of July I went north; destination, Helsinki.

CHAPTER 11

Scandinavian Circuit

The slender spires of Leubeck must have bade many a weary traveller a heartening welcome. Though man-made the city offered sudden change of scenery after twelve hours of some of the dullest country in Europe. Furthermore it was the gateway to the Baltic and a change too in the mode of travel.

A cold wind was blowing as I boarded the ferry boat at Grossenbrode. The regular travellers, particularly the Germans, knew the form here. For the equivalent of ten shillings one could stuff as much Danish *Smorresbrod* under the belt as a twelve hour-starved stomach could hold. It was said that the Germans, with five years of semi-starvation to make up, made the trip to Denmark and back just on this account. True or not many were still wiping *Smorresbrod* remains from their faces as, three hours later, the ship docked at Gedser.

Resumption of the steady beat of train wheels sent most of us straight to sleep and the bustle of Copenhagen station was little more than a disturbed dream. Even the crossing of the Ore Sound with its attendant buffetting and shunting were simply noises in the night. Only as the dawn sun caressed the red roofs of Linkoping did I stir from an unaccustomed lethargy to muse over my proposed operations in Stockholm later in the morning.

With a whole day at my disposal I had ample time to locate the Czech Consulate and effect my business before catching the night boat to Finland. Harbouring no illusions of obtaining even a transit visa inside of a week I intended continuing to Helsinki whatever happened and, if doubtful of the outcome of the Stockholm application, follow it up with another in the Finnish capital.

My briefcase bulged with correspondence between my own firm and Czech import and export concerns in Prague that had been simmering for months. The contacts made had been carefully nourished and had reached a point where, commercially, big things were expected of me. How I was going to unravel myself from various undertakings was going to be a problem in itself, but first things first. I also had letters from Herr Zenk of Vienna proving without doubt that my intention was to continue from Prague to Austria. The big hoodwink was on.

The Holland-Scandinavia Express was due in at Stockholm Central at 9.45 a.m. In actual fact, following a journey of fifty hours from the Hook, it hissed into the Central Station one minute late and my Swedish travelling companion glanced at his watch in profound annoyance. That one brief action personified to me the Swedish mentality. Once, in Gothenburg, I had witnessed a bus passenger upbraiding the driver for dropping him in an outer suburb four minutes behind schedule following a traffic jam in the city centre. Sticklers for time and formality, the Swedes never lose opportunity of flaunting it to all.

Breakfasting on *Smorgasen*, the vast Scandinavian sandwich which has a disconcerting habit of spreading itself on the floor and in one's lap before the remnants reach the mouth, I regirded my loins for battle. I could reward one bouquet to the Swedes anyway. They could offer a better breakfast than some countries I knew.

With the usual navigational difficulties appropriate to a strange city I tracked down the Czechoslovak Embassy and my arrival coincided with the unlocking of the big front door.

The interview with the Consul General himself—for my imposing documents enticed the top man from his lair—got off to a fine start. Under the impression he was dealing with a son of Rothschild I was offered wine and the comfort of his study while the formalities were put in motion. The Consul General shrugged amiably; so much he deprecated the formalities but, as you understand, they just had to be kept. This day and age and all that. Contact Prague? Well—yes, but again a mere formality. Normally it would take ten days but, for me, he would telephone the Department direct. His assistant was doing it now in fact. But his assistant wasn't doing it now in fact. He came in at that moment without knocking and whispered excitedly to his boss. The Consul excused himself and the two hurriedly left the room.

I hardly recognised him when he returned. A scowl had replaced the smile, my passport was thrust back at me and I was curtly informed that a transit visa could not be granted. Somewhere, I thought, they must have a little black book. I turned to go, disappointment flooding into the hope, and wished at least I had drunk more of his damn wine.

Another little nigger boy had gone for a "burton" and the sights of Stockholm turned sour, though for this, the Swedes were not to blame. Scowling at the fashion dummies in the prosperous Kungsgaten I marked time till I could board the evening steamer to Finland.

The paradise of a thousand and one tree-clad islands through which the boat steered an erratic course saved the day from complete depression and the setting sun kindled a succession of fires on the smooth waters of the Stockholm Archipelago. It was a beautiful sight; each little island a haven of tranquillity for a Swedish family escaping from the whirl of weekday life.

It was only the cold night air that drove me below, but upon rising early next morning I perceived that we were still in the Archipelago. But the captain had not lost his way. Instead we were nearing our destination through its Finnish counterpart. A blood-red sunrise above the green Baltic gave me a fitting introduction to a brave little nation.

The dilapidated shipyards of Turku gave evidence of a lack of prosperity such as enjoyed by her rich neighbour, but any ideas of the county being another poverty-stricken Hungary—though they did indeed share a similar language—were quickly dispelled as the ancient but lively bus rattled me into Helsinki; sixty miles and seventy five minutes later.

Rain was falling as we entered the suburbs of the capital, but the banks of storm-clouds above the city failed to dim the aura of the modern elegant buildings that glowed in their own lightness. Reaching the terminus near the impressive Central Station, itself one of the sights of Helsinki, I was delighted to find a friend I had last seen in England awaiting my arrival.

Saimi, blonde, attractive and Finnish, had for six months been a governess to my brother's family before going on to Paris in a similar capacity. Living in a small town in the north she was temporarily staying in Helsinki, an arrangement that suited me most admirably.

To start with she fixed me up with a hotel and then got me to the Czech Embassy without the usual confusion of wrong trains and language conundrums. But it was closed for the week-end. I would have to wait until Monday and looking a shade guiltily at Saimi's trim figure I was quite prepared for her to help me with this too.

Accordingly we became a couple of tourists and "did" the town. We explored the harbour, visited the Parliament building, the National Museum and the Sports Stadium, we strolled down Mannerheim Street gazing at the well-stocked shops and went swimming on Suomenlinna Island in the Archipelago. On the Sunday night we danced at the Spanish Kalastajatorppa Restaurant where the rattle of castanets sounded odd the wrong end of Europe. But for neither of us was the pleasure of each other's company a particularly edifying experience since we were both engaged to absent fiancés. Her's, Jean, was due to join her from France the following week and, since I knew him too, this would at least give me another friend.

At the stroke of ten on Monday I presented myself at the Consulate. Clients were a rarity which was, perhaps, not surprising in a country that lived on the edge of Soviet domination and who practiced neutrality for all they were worth. The young Secretary to whom I was eventually taken remained disconcertingly unimpressed by my commercial "spiel" but could see no reason why a transit visa should not be granted.

"Come back in about a fortnight," he advised.

I shouted more in surprise than indignation. "But I want to go now. Surely it doesn't take fourteen days to stamp a passport!"

The Secretary explained patiently that the application had to go to Prague.

"Couldn't my application be telegraphed or something?" I asked, knowing it could.

The man nodded without enthusiasm. "If you are willing to pay for the service, yes, and in that case it will take only four days. Call again on Thursday."

I rose to leave but was restrained.

"Have you three passport photographs, please?"

I said I hadn't.

"I must have three photographs before I can send the application."

"But you don't telegraph the photographs! Surely my not having them this moment won't cause delay?"

The Secretary was not going to be bulldozed from his book of rules. "The application cannot be made until the photographs are received."

"What time do you close?"

"Two o'clock." The reply held a ring of challenge.

I made a mental calculation. "I could drop them into you this afternoon."

"We close at two o'clock."

I was beginning to dislike this young man.

"I know. But presumably you are still working in the afternoon. I could drop them in the letter-box and so wouldn't disturb you."

The Secretary fell back on his parrot phrase. "I **must** have them by two o'clock."

I realised I was wasting valuable time. Bearing in mind that the consulate was twenty minutes fast walk from the city centre, that I could not understand a word of the lingo, that the first three photographers I visited could not oblige in the stipulated time and the fourth, who could, was in his bath, I think I did pretty well by delivering the precious photographs at four minutes to two.

"Thank you" said the Secretary, "I'll get the application off tomorrow."

"Why not today?" I hurled the words at him.

"The diplomatic post goes at midday. Come back on Friday for your visa."

"But you said **Thursday** before, and—." Words failed me. I departed hurriedly less they returned.

The days of waiting passed pleasantly enough. Most of the time I was alone for Saimi worked during the day and was only free in the evenings. Tiring of the urban attractions of Helsinki I explored further afield, taking advantage of my self-enforced stay to see a little more of a fascinating country.

North-East, along the jagged coastline from the capital lay Porvoo, a small township of waterfront chalet-type houses. Built on the slope of a hill the houses looked as if they were about to tumble into the river below. Even if they had the occupants would have remained dry because of the density of logs covering the water's surface. I was invited to try my hand at log-punting and was lucky to escape with no more than a wet foot.

Another journey took me to Hameenlinna on the edge of the Tampere lake chain. A colourful market town, it lay within the great silence of the Finnish lake country; country that held tragedy and heroism in its very air and glory in its vastness. Looking at it in the knowledge that it continued unchanged except in detail for hundreds of miles, it was easy to appreciate where Sibelius obtained inspiration for his great symphonies.

With the arrival in Helsinki of Saimi's fiance in the middle of the week I acquired a companion. Together we explored the neighbourhood of Pirkkala and wondered why we could not find the naval base that, until recently, had been Soviet property. Later we discovered the base to be spelt Porkkala! Accepting a challenge by Jean I sampled the ferocious extremes of temperature in a village sauna bath and had to submit to the unabashed attentions of the sauna queen herself who had me stretched out naked on a red hot slab while she alternately massaged my body and emptied buckets of ice-cold water over it.

Optimistically I called at the Consulate on the Thursday, but the Secretary was determined to have his pound of flesh. Again I was his first customer Friday morning.

He was full of the joys of Spring. "Good morning Mr. Portway," he began cheerfully, "yes, I'm pleased to say we have received your visa decision from Prague. He sounded agreeably surprised that the Prague Government acknowledged his remote existence.

I waited.

The Secretary cleared his throat as if to make a pronouncement of world-wide import.

"I have the honour to inform you that my Government has come to a decision with regard to your visa application and regrets that it is unable to empower me to grant you a transit visa."

"You mean, no," I said. It wasn't really a disappointment. I suppose in my heart I hadn't expected anything else. Probably my chief emotion was annoyance that the little runt of a Secretary got so much satisfaction out of it. I turned on my heel and left.

The following afternoon I took my leave of Saimi and Jean, of the clean brightness of Helsinki, and the brooding silence of Finland. I sailed in the S.S. Birgar Jarl bound for Stockholm and watched my two friends shrink into the general outline of the harbour. No doubt there were sighs of relief with my parting. Now they could be alone with each other...

Sharing my cabin was an English speaking Norwegian. In spite of scant encouragement he began talking the moment I took possession of my bunk and when I returned later in the evening continued at the exact point he had left off. I took to my bed to an oration upon the glories of Oslo; part three of a recitation upon the magnificence of the country of his birth. Even his snores that followed had a musical Peer Gynt flavour that successfully denied me any hope of sleep.

I lay on the hard bunk staring up at the ventilating duct thinking of Anna. But Oslo kept intruding. How far was the Norwegian capital from Stockholm anyway? I gave myself a lesson in geography and decided to make it a practical one. Norway was a country I'd like to see anyway and though I was fast losing faith in this Embassy lark one might as well, while in Scandinavia, complete the quartet so to speak. So Oslo was added to my itinerary and I could still end up at the Copenhagen consulate on the way home. As the dim light of dawn crept through the port-hole I fell asleep.

A warm sun blazed down upon Stockholm and it was Sunday. It was the combination that, to all Stockholmians, means escape from the bustle of the town. I joined the exodus and so helped transfer the bustle to Drottningholm Palace. But the only polite superlatives I could find for the palace was its size. With pleasure I caught a boat back to the peaceful emptiness of Stockholm.

To save the expense of a hotel I had decided to catch the night train to Oslo. The rhythmic beat of its wheels was more inducible to slumber than the snores of my Norwegian patriot and I awoke, creased but refreshed, in the land of his Fathers.

Perhaps the most unlikely capital city in Europe, after Dublin, is Oslo. Incredibly ugly buildings jostle for prominence among the older, more mellow edifices of history, the whole ungainly mixture surrounded by an aroma of hospitality, charm and fish, which serve to make Oslo one of the most delightful of capitals as well.

Through the good services of the Accommodation Location Service I set up base in an inexpensive but scrupulously clean establishment close to the city centre. The Location Service didn't stretch to Consulates but, with time for once on my side, I contentedly lost myself in a friendly tramway system and eventually ended up in Frederick Nansens Plass. Before ten o'clock I was taking up a position outside a brass plate bearing a lion rampant and the words "*Cesky Konsulat*".

The fact that banks and consulates throughout the world seem addicted to British pub hours is probably irrelevant. Nevertheless on the stroke of ten the "Czech Arms" opened its doors.

Right from the start the interview went with a swing. Again my qualifications brought forth the Consul General himself and within a minute his office was awash with pamphlets, catalogues and letters of introduction. I obtained the impression that their man in Oslo had more of a flair for business than for the Diplomatic Service and I could only hope that neither vocation was nipped in the bud by his flamboyant gesture of granting me a transit visa without reference to his Managing Directors.

With unbelieving eyes I stared at the latest mauve stamp in my passport. Energetically shaking my benefactor by the hand I almost ran out of his office in case someone turned up with the black book.

The rest of the morning was a pleasant marathon as I worked through various agencies and authorities obtaining the tickets, reservations and permits necessary for a journey to Prague. At a travel agency in the Storgaten I purchased a rail ticket to Copenhagen.

In the B.E.A. offices beneath the squat red-brick towers of Oslo's vast bunker of a Town Hall I tried to effect a reservation on the weekly flight Copenhagen-Berlin-Prague. Cussedness crept in from another quarter here when I was told that this could only be arranged in Copenhagen. Since, to complete the other arrangements, I had to know which day I would be flying it was important that confirmation be effected immediately etc., etc.... Yes, they had heard of an instrument called a telephone, but... Leaving this detail to the Gods I returned to Fred Nansens and, before the pubs closed in Britain for the afternoon, rapped on the iron-studded door of the Soviet Embassy, a pretentious, palace-like affair rivalling in size the Royal Castle. My summons produced a sour Russian who spoke only his native tongue. Reinforcements between them could muster Norwegian, Bulgarian, Ukranian, Swedish and Kurdish; all incomprehensible to me. Finally a Norwegian floor-scrubber was pressed into service who came up trumps with well-nigh Harrovian English! But my request for a transit visa allowing me to land and take-off from Schoenfeld Airport outside Berlin produced nothing more than a ditty on Soviet non-interference in the affairs of the German Democratic Republic. Since the G.D.R. was not represented in Norway I saw difficulties so left this one likewise in the hands of the gods. The despatch of a telegram to Anna completed the morning's chores, and the picked backbone of an enormous fish bore mute evidence of a well-earned and satisfied appetite.

Before I caught my night train to Copenhagen I had ample time for a boat trip up the broad sheltered waters of Oslo Fjord. With one hurdle behind me I tried to turn my attention to the next once I was in Czechoslovakia, but the prospect of seeing Anna eclipsed serious deliberation. Instead I was content to leave it until we were together. A lot could be done in forty eight hours.

The lights of Oslo slid into the early darkness of a Northern night as my train carried me south. Long would I remember the Norwegian capital with gratitude. Unkindly I slept through the full length of Western Sweden and awoke to see the squat silhouette of Kronborg Castle at Elsinore upholding a long defunct command of the Ore Sound. The huge spread of suburban Copenhagen starts from its legendary walls though it was more than forty minutes before we drew into the crowded Central Station to add to the morning rush hour.

The gods had not let me down when I came to book my seat on the Czech C.S.A.* flight OK.432 out of Kastrup. In fact the joke was on

*Czechoslovak State Airline.

me for only two seats had been taken! I left the Airways Office in Hans Christian Anderson's Boulevard scattering a flock of pigeons in my relief.

Three hours later I reported in at Kastrup Airport. Even through my optimism I could not but notice, as I passed through the capable hands of the Danish Immigration and Customs Authorities, that Flight OK.432 was something of an enigma, a mystery flight to the unknown. "Nobody ever returns from 432; they just go with passive submission and never come back" the driver of my airport bus had told me. Twice a Passport Officer checked my nationality and credentials while an airways official queried with some incredulity my destination. By the time I was walking across the windswept tarmac to the Czech Dakota standing alone shunned, as it were, by the other aircraft I became infected by this strange dread. I even found myself wanting to run back to the friendly Danes silently watching the departure but, chiding myself, pressed on in company with my two fellow passengers; a couple of minor diplomats wrapped in fur collared overcoats. Anyone would have thought we were going to Siberia! I winced. Maybe we were!

Selecting a seat midway up the fuselage I settled down to enjoy the two hour hop to Berlin conscious of the stares of the air hostess. The red warning light came on illuminating the "fasten safety belts" notice in Czech and I fumbled for a strap that was not there. Catching the hostess's eye, she shrugged helplessly in what may have been apology or derision and I didn't even bother to move to another seat.

The old Dakota shook itself and flapped into the air clawing for height as it skimmed the choppy Baltic. No safety belts, no barley sugar and only "Rude Pravo" and the "Daily Worker"* to read. Flight OK.432 was definitely one to be avoided I thought with grim amusement. What would the Gods have in store for me at Schoenfeld? Then for the second time I began to ponder upon what I was setting out to do in Prague. And with only forty eight hours to do it—the gods would really have to work overtime.

Down below our shadow raced across the flat Mecklenburg countryside.

*Now the "Morning Star."

CHAPTER 12

Mixed Blessings

Travel-sickness is a state of mind they say. But it was more than my mind that was in a state. Somewhere over Neubrandenburg where, as airline captains euphemistically put it, we entered a "pocket of turbulence". For no apparent reason the ancient aircraft dipped and tossed and flung itself about the sky.

I tried the age-old adage of not watching a reeling skyline, I tried holding my breath, counting sheep; anything to counteract the growing nausea in my stomach. But all to no avail. Accepting the inevitable I groped for the "spew bag" but, being flight 432, of course, there wasn't one. "Rude Pravo" saved the immediate situation but my expensive Copenhagen lunch was hardly to be contained by all the reading matter at my disposal. Beseechingly I turned pain-racked eyes to the hostess. She was talking to the two other passengers at the back and judging by their glances at me I was the subject under discussion. I couldn't have cared less but was gratified to see my administrating angel detach herself and come my way.

"May I see your passport please." She demanded hovering above me at a great height.

I could hardly believe my ears. Groping for the thing in a daze I opened my mouth to beg the necessary requisites for being sick in an aircraft but had to shut it quick again.

While she studied the passport my eyes caught sight of the two diplomats—or were they policemen?—sitting impassively like twin ghouls watching my misery. It was obviously they who had put the girl up to this. I burped loudly in their direction.

"But you haf no transit visum for the *Deutsche Demokratische Republik*," the voice above me bleated in a tone that pronounced the eclipse of the universe.

I turned a water-filled eye up to her. "I'm not going to Germany."

"But we land at Berlin and you cannot land at Berlin," she argued, probing for rarely-used English.

I was in no mood to argue. "O.K. I'll go on alone," I said and relapsed into a coma. And then I could hold it no longer. My warning cry went unheeded, as I deposited the second course of my lunch over the lady's sleeve. The unfortunate girl retreated at speed towards her cabin in the rear all argument forgotten. I felt a lot better.

The firm grass runway of Schoenfeld was a balm to my ills and the fresh breeze that cut across the flight apron cleared my head in seconds. The air hostess had had no time to resume her lecture on the impossibility of landing in the G.D.R. with no transit visa and, with some trepidation, ushered her flock of three past a parade of Volkspolizei standing rigidly to attention in full battle kit. For one fanciful moment I wondered if my fame as a business-man had gone that far, and then I saw, walking down the middle column, hand at the salute, a Russian army officer of substantial rank and girth, carrying out an inspection. A bevy of lesser mortals of correspondingly less braid and padding trotted nervously at his heels.

In the transit lounge I was left to my own devices amongst a small crowd of nervous fellow "transitees" awaiting their tannoyed instructions. Nobody at all wanted to see the assortment of papers we all clutched which was probably the reason for the general air of nervousness. It certainly wasn't the G.D.R. I knew and a loud-mouthed American Communist who, a minute ago, had been lauding the industrial five-year-plan querulously asked the assembly whether he'd been dropped in the wrong zone. The huge murals around the lounge walls depicting East German industrial might should have comforted him.

The announcement of the resumption of the Prague flight was occasion for a general exodus. Blessing the fat Russian General with all my heart for occupying the attention of his German minions I climbed aboard the old Dakota. The air hostess pointedly produced a paper bag, handed it to me and retired to a safe distance.

It was only a short hop to Prague; not even time in fact to make use of my equipment. Through the window I watched the Czech capital move sideways past the window and the evening sun splash red on the rocks of Sarka. The runways of Ruzyne Airport rushed to meet us.

My eyes searched the crowded visitors' enclosure as we walked to immigration but did not see her. I handed over my passport, still searching.

"You will be staying at the Alcron." The voice of the plain-clothes man distracted me.

"Oh no, nothing ritzy like that," I replied, knowing the Alcron to be one of Prague's largest hotels catering for foreigners.

"You will be staying at the Alcron," repeated the man and I awoke to the fact that he was not asking a question.

"Yes," I said without the slightest intention of doing so.

"Furthermore, you will remain in Prague except for the purpose of leaving the Republic, which you must do in any case, within forty eight hours. Is that understood?"

"Yes," I said again. Methods by which I could obtain an extension began to occupy my mind.

Changing some pounds sterling into crowns I retrieved my case and passed out of the arrival bay into the arms of Anna.

Right from the start I became a profound sympathiser of Cinderella. She only had until midnight to burn her candles but my fate was likely to be worse than having my somewhat crumpled suit turn into sack-cloth.

Our meeting had been a pleasant shock. I had hoped she would be at Ruzyne to meet me but the fact that she was took me by surprise. Pessimism had become my second name.

"Have a good flight darling?" Anna had tenderly enquired.

I never could produce a speech of greeting. "I was sick," I told her.

In all we tried nine hotels. Eight of them had vacant rooms but, upon seeing my British passport, managed to find excuses for denying me a room. The ninth was the Alcron.

In the morning we took a gamble. Risking three of our precious forty-eight hours I made a whistle-stop tour of the various commercial enterprises I had contacted and struck oil at the fourth. In return for the sale to "Motokov"* of one of the patent oil-fired boilers made by my firm they would grant me a certificate that would prolong my stay. This, in effect, was the bargain and though I knew they would copy the product I didn't think they'd get very far on Soviet oil.† Most of the afternoon was spent in police stations obtaining another stamp in my passport but, hour for hour, we chalked up forty to our credit.

Next we broke the rules and, in a taxi, drove the thirty five kilometres to Anna's home. Making sure we were not being followed we settled down to talk treason again discussing, in an aura of unreality, the most desperate venture an engaged couple had surely ever embarked upon. We talked calmly, lightheartedly, almost as if making our next date.

Oddly it was not Austria, East Germany or Hungary upon which our new venture was based. A new country had come into our growing

*The State import agency for mechanical appliances.
†They didn't!

107

vocabulary of escape—Poland. To Anna the mountainous district of the Slovak-Polish border provided a clean, more natural way out. Moreover she knew the district a little and had recently done her homework by taking a week's holiday in the High Tatra's near Javorina. Encouraged by her enthusiasm I took over from there. With Poland a simmering ferment of broken revolution* and a new liberalisation sweeping the country it should not be difficult for me to meet her there and, together, make our way to the East German border. Even here my new-found optimism did not falter. I remembered from years before a section of the River Oder below Frankfurt where the waters were shallow... or, if this way out to Berlin was barred then there were ships at Stettin or Gdansk.

In the cosy living-room of Anna's home, which I saw for the first time, I met again her mother and father. I had seen them briefly at Lidice the previous year but marvelled afresh at the silent adoration they lavished upon their daughter. It made our task all the harder for the retribution it would certainly bring them. Then and there we decided to give it just one more year and, should the forces of reason make no headway, the "Polish plan", as we called it, would go into effect in August 1957. In the meantime I would myself visit, if I could, the Polish side of the border around Javorina and Zakopane and also continue my efforts to visit Anna.

Putting further deliberations behind us Anna and I tried to spend the remainder of the day more normally as is fitting an engaged couple visiting the home of the bride. But bizarre situations simply refused to leave us in peace. Halfway through the afternoon, in spite of our secret arrival an agitated man rushed into the house like a frightened rabbit burbling something about an important report to make to the Englander. It turned out that he was a friend of my future father-in-law (which explained the leakage for he could never keep a secret!) and wanted to inform me of the fact that a Soviet rocket unit had recently taken up positions in the woods close to the nearby village of Msec. He wanted me to come and see for myself but I had enough troubles without getting involved in espionage. I knew the woods in question so, after getting all the details I could out of him, promised to report the matter to the competent authorities. It was supposed that there were no Russian forces in Czechoslovakia so I appreciated the piece of intelligence could be important and, since I intended seeing the British Consul in the morning anyway,

---

*In June of that year (1956) the Poznan uprising had occurred, order being restored only by the use of tanks.

108

I decided to pass this report to the military attache at the same time.

With my original forty-eight hours exhausted Anna and I returned to Prague and the impersonal care of the Alcron Hotel. A man in the foyer jumped perceptively as we entered the foyer and a look of relief crossed his face as if pleased that he had found us again.

The British Consul could offer but cold comfort the following day. Yes, of course he would continue to press the Czech Authorities for Anna's release but... there were too many "buts" in the discourse for my liking . . . the interview with the military attache—a colonel of, I think, the Warwicks—was at least more entertaining.

Having introduced myself rank-name-and-number-wise, I opened my mouth to make my rocket report and closed it again on being passed a scrap of paper which read "Write it down and talk only small-talk". So scribbling away madly I attempted to split my mind into the technicalities of ballistic missiles on one hand and the vagaries of Czech weather on the other. If either the report or the conversation made sense I would be surprised!

Finishing my essay the colonel and I spoke briefly on imagined mutual acquaintances in Colchester. Then he beckoned me outside and in the Embassy Courtyard explained that his office was "bugged" but that it was convenient to feed the opposition with false information.

Our remaining day in Prague was spent in discussing details of the "Polish plan" (though not in the hotel in case this too was bugged!) and watching the hands of the clock inexorably creeping round to a quarter to midnight, the departure time of my train. We wore ourselves out walking aimlessly around the city and subjecting our bruised and battered hearts to as much torture as our feet. The man who followed us only had his feet to worry about.

At the Central Station I boarded my southbound express on stolen time for even my extension had run out. But whereas Cinderella paid the price by the loss of a dress and a pumpkin coach I was losing a princess. She was crying now as I kissed her goodbye lightheartedly with a joke on my lips. It was the best way.

The train crawled out of the station and into the adjoining tunnel. The momentary darkness was as a protecting cloak and the only witness to my own grief.

CHAPTER 13

Polish Plan

The prodding of a dozing viper is a pastime not recommended to those wishing to live a quiet and orderly existence. Dozing vipers have a not unnatural habit of waking up and doing a little prodding themselves. Furthermore, vipers have poison tongues.

For nearly four years I had been prodding the vicious serpent of a Communist state. I had been rebuffed, obstructed and repelled. I had been ticketed, docketed and declared persona non grata. I had probed its long bloated body from all directions by land and in the air. I had assaulted it head on and the forked tongue had threatened me, and I had crept up behind to be lashed at by its tail.

Now, as another autumn tinted the old wych-elm, the angry viper uncoiled and struck back. And the barbed tongue was poison indeed.

I had been back in Britain no more than a month when I was invited to Westminster by Fenner Brockway. Over a cup of tea and a bun in the Members' canteen I listened in angry silence to a list of "proven misdeeds" attributed to my fiancee and perpetrated over the last two years. In short, Anna was alleged to be two-timing me.

The accusations, still fresh and vitriolic from the lips of the ambassador of the Czechoslovak Republic, and repeated now in a quiet neutral voice by a highly respected member of the British Parliament, poured into my astounded ears. No doubt some of the seed was supposed to fall upon fertile ground but the picture my mind conjured up of senior governmental officials and high-ranking diplomats issuing communiques and furnishing reports on the tittle-tattle of a small country town was absurd enough to kill all seeds stone dead.

Altogether this amazing ambassadorial comedy was acted out three times over a period of two months, by which time the imaginative powers of the local authorities presumably dried up.

Even had I no immediate explanation for some of Anna's "indiscretions" the ludicrous proceedings were so clumsily carried out as to be an obvious fake. This surprised me for the Czechs were capable of better deception than that. But I knew my Anna and though our physical acquaintanceship over four years could be measured only in days we had, together, touched both the depths and the heights of human emotion.

Your fiancee's clothes, they said, were fashionable and expensive, only obtainable in the most exclusive salons of Prague. What they did not know was that the source of some of the material was Britain; nor had they knowledge of Anna's very considerable skill as a dressmaker.

Likewise the holiday in the Tatra Mountains of Slovakia. Surely an extravagance beyond the means of a non-working girl? The implication made me smile. I could hardly announce to her accusers the reason for that visit!

A skiing session in company with soldiers of the Czech Army could produce no immediate explanation but neither could it afford me any loss of sleep. I did know however that Anna's home adjoined a large barracks.

Another embryo accusation was strangled at birth by Anna herself. Followed in the train to Prague one day by two known S.T.B. men one of them clumsily invited her to the cinema with him. His overtures were tartly rejected but had, through fear, she submitted, no doubt another "indiscretion" would have been added to the list.

I awarded the booby prize to the accusation concerning the late-night debauchery attributed to Anna and a tall young man in a Prague night club. Even dates and times and a wealth of detail were available proving without doubt that it was I who was the secret lover!

Other less specific instances of Anna's apparent disloyalty I treated with the contempt they deserved and some of the shame of the sordid little business wiped off on to poor Fenner Brockway who was as glad as I was when this insidious method of attack was finally revoked.

In far less diplomatic fashion the British Press clumsily came to my aid with headlines in the inner pages proclaiming "Reds Hold Fiancee", "Iron Curtain Romance Frustrated by Red Government" and gems of a similar nature. Appreciating both the value of the Press but also its tendency to lurid exaggeration, particularly in view of the Czech Ambassador's insinuation that his help was conditional upon no press coverage, I attempted to get the reporters off my back. Unsuccessful, I spent two consecutive nights in the clamorous offices of two London newspapers trying to tone down the volume. I might as well have spent them in bed.

Even quicker off the mark were my Intelligence friends who promptly summoned me to the "War House" hardly had I set foot in my own after my return from Prague. But I refused to be summoned on this occasion and the Mountain had to come to Mahommed to glean further pickings from my rocket report. Later a Czech working for British Intelligence came to see me but again it was my vulner-ability to blackmail that worried him and both my father and I had quite a fight to maintain my commission in the Territorial Army.

But this last pin prick hurt little; indeed it was, in a way, a comfort to know that the faceless-ones of Security were watching my every move. Come August 1957 and it might be good to have them around.

Those on the other side came for her again as the first cold fingers of winter spread across the land. Anna was taking in the washing when the two S.T.B. appeared at the back gate of her home. No-one saw her go.

Outside police-headquarters, a friend observed her being hustled from the car, and it dawned upon Anna that this slender link could be the only means of communication with her family should she not return.

But again she was allowed to leave. The interview, conducted by a senior member of the organisation was short. He was polite and as cold as the embryo winter. His warning was ugly.

As with trembling fingers Anna removed the last of the washing from the line she knew the writing on the wall could be no plainer. Even a child could read that she would not remain at liberty far into 1957.

Sensing the danger spiralling towards its vortex I lost no time in resuming my nefarious schemes. Though we had named August of the following year as our "D Day" neither of us was going to quibble should circumstances warrant advancement of the date by a month or so. Accordingly I brought out, for re-appraisal, the idea that had lain in cold storage at the back of my mind.

A visit to Poland, even an individual one, was now no great problem so that aspect of the "Polish plan" was not in jeopardy. But though she knew the district a little I was not happy about letting Anna make her own way across treacherous inhospitable mountains to a tiny dot on the map which would be our rendezvous on Polish territory. I also knew my fiancee's navigational abilities which gave real cause for concern! No, if the new scheme was to go ahead I would accompany her over the physical barrier.

For a start the scheme called for a forged passport. In support of this requirement I possessed a batch of expired and exhausted passports thoughtfully returned by a considerate Foreign Office. Also a somewhat flamboyant friend of my soldiering days whose artistic talents covered the range from interior decoration to the "touching up" of legal documents. I went to see Tom at his rambling old ruin of a home in Suffolk but before he could go to work an even better slice of luck came my way. A school-friend afflicted with similar features to my own re-entered my life just at this juncture. Equipped with his passport and using his name I foresaw no visa difficulties anywhere.

As my mind sifted both the problems and the permutations of the scheme new possibilities emerged. Not only would I be able to get a perfectly legitimate visa for Poland but also one for Czechoslovakia. For East Germany, travelling east to west, it would be necessary to obtain a transit visa from Warsaw but this again would be a formality.

Suitably disguised as my school friend and using his passport Anna could openly leave her country, travel through Poland and out through East Germany to the sanctuary of West Berlin. The passport would contain, as well as a full complement of visas, the correct number of entry stamps obtained by me up to the point of handover.

But what about me? Here the solution was a little less sure. Reverting to my own passport which, though adequately visa'd for Poland, would be inadequately stamped since I would have to enter Poland illegally. I would follow Anna after a suitable interval. By way of the mountains I would get as far as possible along the escape route before running into trouble over the missing stamps. Thereafter I should have to fall back on either a lost passport procedure or my own simple escape bid via the Oder shallows at Frankfurt or one of the Baltic ports. But by that time Anna would be out and, to me, this was all that mattered.

The initial route for both of us had to be via the mountains—the Tatra mountains—of Slovakia and Poland, for the Czech border was the weakest link in the chain. But the check-point at Javorina was little-used and therefore they were not likely to scrutinize Anna's bona fides too thoroughly while, for me, a border running through an inhospitable mountain range would be ill-defined and scantily guarded. For the execution of the final phase of the plan Anna would await my arrival at an address in West Berlin and, failing my appearance by a certain date, was to surrender herself to the Federal Authorities.

My school-friend readily agreed to the loan of his passport even at the considerable risk of losing it. The photograph only needed a few artistic touches and a little "blurring"; chicken-feed to the capable Tom.

A visit to a well-known Haymarket firm of wig and gown-makers for the acting profession produced the where-with-all to transform Anna's dark Slavonic features into a more Anglo-Saxon complexion. Much explanation was necessary and since I had no intention of telling him the true reasons for my requirements the wretched salesman must have thought he was dealing with a madman. The size and shape of Anna's head was a vital statistic and my fiancee too must have wondered why on earth I should choose that moment to buy her a hat!

In the middle of October I applied, in my friend's name, for a Czech visa. With the application I sent his passport and a typed letter, signed by him, explaining the reason for making so early an application. I would be out of the country for much of the time I said but would have to go to Prague almost immediately upon returning to London.

Next my wig arrived together with a box of grease paints, creams and adhesives. I looked out a suit and various outer male garments too small for me but which might, in parts, fit Anna.

A week later I received notification from my friend (whose Buckinghamshire address I was also using) that a request for a visa had to be accompanied by the applicant. Not without some qualms he was persuaded to present himself at the Embassy in Notting Hill Gate leaving me, offering moral encouragement and practicing a new signature on the beer mats, at a pub down the road. Within an hour he returned, greatly relieved.

The preliminaries completed I settled down to sweat out the waiting. Sometime before our "D Day" I would fit in a visit to Poland. Once or twice I pondered upon the price of failure of the scheme. The consequences would be dire and heaven knows how many countries besides my own would fling the book at us!

Then on the 22nd October came a diversion. That morning in far-off Hungary a page of history began to turn and the world watched enthralled as the flames of revolt spread from Budapest to engulf a country stricken by Communism.

In company with millions of my own countrymen I listened in admiration to the reports of savage acts of retribution being performed in the Hungarian capital and, when Budapest Radio broadcast its desperate cries for help as Soviet tanks began quelling the rebellion with equal savagery, the admiration turned to shame. But in my case I had a personal reason for the shame. Here was an opportunity not only to strike a blow for a brave people but also to use the chaos of war to enter neighbouring Czechoslovakia. Instead, fettered by convention and indecision, I waited inert while the grim drama was played out.

Only when, out of the blue, there came a letter from a London University student organisation did I stir my stumps. It asked in matter-of-fact tones whether I would be prepared, with my wartime military and evasion experiences coupled with a more recent knowledge of conditions in Hungary, to put these assets at the disposal of the patriots in the shrapnel-torn streets of Budapest.

I said yes and followed it up with a visit to the organising secretary, a dangerously dedicated young man. As a result I was "promoted" to the "advisory committee" where, in company, with an ex-paratroop major and another Hungarian "expert", I found myself saddled with a multitude of problems not the least of which involved the technicalities of blowing up sections of the Hungarian State Railway.

I began to lose faith in the venture when, a few days later, the first of a series of missives reached me announcing week-end hikes on Dartmoor as a form of training while, in direct contradiction, two midnight telephone calls instructed me to get dressed and report to an address in Vienna.

My growing suspicion of the whole affair fortunately delayed my departure long enough to receive the cancellation messages that followed, and whilst the potential freedom fighters were presumably frolicking in the Devon heather, the grim tragedy in Hungary was played out to its inevitable finale.

Hardly had the flames died in Budapest when I found the opportunity to visit Poland. Their embassy in Langham Place granted the visa with disconcerting promptitude and, in my car, I set off for Zakopane and the Tatra Mountains. By car it would be easier to make a less conspicuous reconnaissance.

Travelling eastwards the East German transit visa was but a tiresome formality at the border control beyond Helmstedt. Stuffing the car with petrol and myself with victuals beforehand I made Frankfurt-on-Oder without stopping and, from Slubice on the Polish side, made a brief examination of the Oder shallows below the Frankfurt suburb of Damm Vorstadt. The shallows were less than my memory had indicated but the current was sluggish, and in the summer, the river would be no great impediment. The peaceful countryside of woods and fields offered no signs of Polish frontier defences but, in a Slubice *bierhaus*, I learnt of intensive patrolling on the German shore.

Turning southwards I reached Wroclaw[1] next morning and, in its still ruined streets foraged for supplies and information. As in Yugoslavia I found my car buried beneath a sea of admirers upon my return. I camped out that night in the dreary coalmining district of Stalinograd[2] where, twelve years before as a prisoner of war, I had been a slave miner of the German Reich. I could not resist a visit to Hindenburg[3] and my coalmine the following day and though previously neither the Polish Embassy or the Ministry of Mines in Warsaw could offer me any encouragement I presented myself not-withstanding at the local Trade Union Office with the request that I make an inspection of my old stamping ground. Met with some surprise and courtesy my personal intervention failed to reverse the decision and since Communist industry is, in itself, an armed camp I expected nothing less.

They couldn't stop me looking at the place from the road however and a demand from a Britisher to see the *Direktor* at the main gate was such a rare request to the squad of Worker's Militia guarding it that the great man himself arrived to see what the fuss was about. He was made of sterner stuff than the clerks of the Trade Union and, upon learning of my connection with the mine, offered me the complete Cook's tour.

It was an eerie experience to don mining gear again, to descend at speed into the bowels of the earth and to walk the eternal subterranean tunnels. In the main gallery at the base of the lift-shaft a press conference was held in my honour and I was invited to comment upon the improvements in working conditions as opposed to those of twelve years before. I had to be careful with my words here but could presume that Communist miners were fed adequately which was more than could be said for those under the Germans!

A hot shower, a half tumbler of slivovice and I resumed my journey with just one brief halt at Oswiecim to see again the well-preserved horror of Auschwitz Concentration Camp. I dallied too for a few hours amongst the ancient buildings of Cracow making up for an omission in 1944 when the railway yards and Gestapo Headquarters had been all I had seen of this historic city. It was late in the evening when I pulled into Zakopane.

To my mind Zakopane, from a tourist angle, is a disappointment. The great mountains of the Tatra range make an inspiring backcloth

---

*1 Formerly Breslau, Capital of Silesia.
*2 Since reverted to its original name of Katowice.
*3 Now Zabrze.

to the little resort but most are in Slovakia. After a night of comfort in a holiday hotel I took the road up the valley away from the cluster of chalets, passed the bitter cold waters of the lake at Kuznice and, where the road was defeated by the gradient, I left the car to continue on foot. Immediately above towered the rocky magnificence of a peak called Kasprowy Wierch. Its southern flank was in Slovakia. A journey by cable car to its summit served to prove that frontier guards were hardly a practical proposition in a region where nature had provided a barrier of its own. Occasional patrols, I was told, went out in the known tourist haunts but......a shrug of the shoulders gave eloquent comment.

Later I drove round the mass of Kasprowy Wierch to little Javorina, the Slovak border post, a mountain torrent forming the frontier. Most of the houses of the village were on the Slovak side huddled round the single lane bridge. To gauge reaction I tried to cross it. The Polish soldier waved me through without a murmur and the Czech guard, unsure of himself, would have caused no fuss either. Only a Czech officer, emerging from the guard room, knew the rules and the very fact he used the Communist greeting *"Praci Cest"* ("Honour to work") precluded any hope of a short cut through the formalities. However the incident did show the degree of laxity that existed on this particular border.

Continuing along the road that remained in Polish territory I came to the lake of Morske Oko, a favourite tourist attraction in summer. Its sombre waters reflected the rocky walls of the giant saucer in which it was built and a slippery footpath invited me up to a smaller and higher lake called Czarny Stam. The footpath beckoned again but I knew I was very close to the frontier line and had no wish to draw attention to myself. Here, if anywhere, was my passage out of Czechoslovakia. I took some photographs, made a few calculations and left.

Within ten days of leaving I was home again my reconnaissance mission completed. Optimism radiated from me. The journey across the mountains into Poland would be a piece of cake. I wasn't perhaps quite so sure of the next bit but didn't let it bother me. Anna was the one to be got out without fuss. I'd stumble along after her somehow.

My optimism took a knock when I read a subsequent letter from the Czech Embassy in reply to my friend's visa application. Its familiar phrasing told a familiar story. Possibly my friend's likeness to me was a little too apparent!

CHAPTER 14

Danish Dilemma

Webers Hotel is an unpretentious but comfortable establishment in the Vesterbrogade, very near the centre of Copenhagen. Its friendly fug offered warm welcome as I passed through the revolving doors from the cold, snow-swept street outside. At the reception desk I completed the registration formalities, my numb fingers fumbling with the pen, and collecting my key together with a letter, addressed to me, I followed the receptionist up a single flight of stairs to my room.

Left alone I tore open the envelope and, as I scanned the contents, a slight frown of disappointment clouded my face. Mild guilt grappled momentarily with the disappointment resulting from the knowledge that the writer would be unable to join me in a cosy little dinner I had planned for that evening. A pity, for in addition to being young and pretty, she had earned it and more. The letter was signed "Christine".

All of which requires a little explaining.

Acquaintanceships born on a train journey seldom blossom longer than the journey's length and in spite of well-intentioned pledges of eternal friendship the thing usually dies with the mad scramble for luggage and station exit at journey's end. This particular acquaintanceship, however, born on the west-bound Austria Express eighteen months previously, miraculously survived the bustle of Ostend terminus.

Returning from Hungary I had, with some prompting, unfolded some of my troubles to a sympathetic Christine who, making a first and lone trip to England from her native Denmark, seemed in need of diversionary conversation to keep a worried mind off the ominous prospect of encountering the wily Briton en masse in their lairs. Safely escorted into the care of her English sponsors she pledged her desire to help should she ever be in a position to do so.

And there the matter would have ended had not I, looking for a way to make one final legal visit to Czechoslovakia to deliver, with full explanations, the props and disguises appertaining to the "Polish Plan", remembered Christine's pledge. She **was** in a position to help. Copenhagen was the one suitable European capital remaining whose Czech Consulate had not occasion to have had anything to do with me. And with the encouraging performance of Oslo still a warm memory, it was an omission worth rectifying.

The fact that the Czechs had unaccountably turned down my school friend's visa application was not of disastrous consequence.

It would only mean that, for both of us, a journey across the mountains would be necessary. We should have to revert to the original idea of effecting a rendezvous in the foothills on the Slovak side returning to Poland together. Since I would come direct to Poland in the first instance and would therefore obtain en route the necessary stamps in **one** of the passports Anna could then proceed normally from Polish territory. But a lot of vitally important arrangements, which could not be trusted to letters, together with delivery of the disguise was important prior to the plan becoming action.

To rush, helter-skelter, to Copenhagen and knock at the big front door of the consulate was an unreliable way of doing things. Instead, I decided to play it a way that would bring more certain dividends. Again I would use the commercial approach.

So, soon after my return from Poland, I invited Christine to become my "post office" in Denmark. She was as good as her word and, for weeks on end, I was able to represent myself as a British businessman temporarily domiciled in Denmark. Reposting my letters and catalogues I gave such a good account of myself and the firm I represented that before long the bait was taken and the Czech Commercial Attache in Copenhagen invited me to visit him to arrange a visit to his country. Christmas had come and gone and the new year of 1957 was two months old when, once more, I left the English shores.

Which offers perfectly good reason why, in a late February blizzard, I should arrive in Copenhagen with a briefcase containing a mass of technical literature, an expensive blonde wig, numerous pots of mysterious creams and a suit several sizes too small for me, not to mention a letter spurning my invitation to one of the prettiest girls in Denmark.

A cold but clear and sunny morning made the search and location of the Czechoslovak Consulate in a select district called Svanemollevej a pleasure. My impatient footsteps ensured I was outside the ivy-covered building within minutes of the usual opening time.

My reception by the commercial attache was, if anything, warmer than that received from his Oslo colleague. He was a long, thin individual, the few hairs on his head carefully trained to cover a premature baldness. His eyes flashed enthusiasm as we discussed the

Czech iron founding business—a subject on which I had done my homework. With some misgivings I accepted an invitation to visit a locomotive works in Ostrava and, to the usual platitudes, completed the required forms.

Leaving me with a cup of black coffee he took my documents into the neighbouring office to return ten minutes later cooing like a midwife following her first delivery. There, on the last page or the battered passport, reposed the results of his artistry, a mauve stamp that aroused in me as much pleasure as twins to a sterile wife. In a welter of fond farewells I passed out into the clean sunshine to make a bee-line for the airways terminal in the city centre.

By midday I was the possessor of a flight ticket and reservation on an old friend, OK 432, departing for Berlin and Prague that very afternoon. The coach ride to Kastrup and the brief formalities at the airport were the mixture as before.

On board the old Dakota, however, things had improved. Both halves of my safety belt were not only present but even worked. Furthermore we were a crowd of five to on this trip, thus two more than last time. If it were not careful C.S.A. would make a profit! The air hostess looked familiar though a degree more care-worn and two of the heavily overcoated figures at the back I could have sworn were my ghouls of last summer.

The red light up front came on and I was bade "*Upevnete ochranny pas*". The engines surged and we were away. Gathering speed we bumped the full length of the main runway and as the fence at the end rushed towards us a notion struck me that the journey was to be made overland. Discovering a stray air current the machine remembered its true function, the fence grazed the still revolving undercarriage wheels and, a minute later, the Zeeland coast receded behind the starboard propeller.

As usual the Baltic below was grey and uninviting. An early morning sun had failed in its promise and so uniformly grey was the sky that it merged with the sea. For all the difference the aircraft might have been flying upside down. It probably was anyway.

But the distant spires of Stralsund and the mainland of Germany, rode into view the right way up. I felt a warm glow of anticipation and excitement. So rapidly had events occurred that I had not even had time to send Anna a cable. She knew I was in Denmark and, no doubt, guessed the reason. Always I had dreamed of a surprise arrival at the little kitchen of her home which was the hub of the household. Now, through no planning on my part, this dream was going to be given the opportunity of coming true. I lay back in my seat tasting, in my imagination, the first tender moments as I walked into the room...

"Your passport, please." The dream slid from view and I was back in a world of hard facts. The hostess looked down at me coldly.

I fumbled in my jacket pocket and waited for the outburst; going through a mythical countdown as the good lady searched through my passport from cover to cover. I was relieved to note she was not the sour amazon of the previous occasion.

"But you have no visa for the German Democratic Republic!" she exploded. She sounded as if I had boarded her aeroplane with no trousers.

"I'm going to Czechoslovakia, not Germany," I pointed out stiffly.

"Yes, but we land at Berlin," she went on in a voice charged with emotion. To her the divided German capital must have been the gateway to heaven.

Unable to take refuge in the messy convulsions of sickness I fell back on a good wholesome lie.

"Both your Ambassador and your Commercial Attache in Copenhagen gave me their word that the transit formalities would be waived on this occasion. I have important business in Prague."

The outrageous statement appeared to mollify the girl and she moved across to her less provocative charges. I sunk back into the dreamworld arms of Anna.

The aircraft lurched suddenly, leaving my stomach transfixed to a cloud, and banked steeply. The red light up front flashed its cryptic message. Retrieving my abdomen I looked out of the window at Berlin lying on its side.

Schoenfeld was still the poor relation of the city's three* airports. It lacked the impressive terminal buildings, general air of efficiency and even the concrete runways of Tempelhof and Tegel. It was also furthest from the centre; being outside the Berlin ring. Hence the need for transit visas.

This last fact was bothering me now as the Dakota rolled its way over the tyre-scarred grass. Walking down the steps the feeling of nakedness assailed me again. There was no Vopo parade this time to

*The fourth, Gatow, is a military airfield.

distract attention from my deficiencies.

The five of us gained the barrier and I noticed the silent group of policemen standing by it. They seemed to be waiting for somebody. My fellow travellers passed through unmolested and I followed trying not to flaunt a guilty conscience.

I started to walk through the gap in the barrier but found my way barred by one of the policemen. He raised a hand to his cap in a polite salute.

"You are Mr. Portway?" he asked in good English.

I replied that I was.

"Then, please, I must ask you to come with me," he continued.

"Why? What have I done?" I demanded, waxing indignation partly to hide my alarm.

"We will not keep you long, sir. Please, be so kind." The policeman turned on his heel knowing I would follow. His two colleagues took up a position on each side of me to ensure I was "kind enough".

In a spacious office I was introduced to a cross-looking civilian who turned out to be a representative of the Czechoslovak Embassy in Berlin.

He came straight to the point.

"Mr. Portway, you not go to Prague, you go back. You understand, yes."

"No," I said understanding him only too well.

Against a background of clattering typewriters the ill-tempered minor diplomat deigned to supply a few explanations. It seemed the granting of my visa in Copenhagen had been a mistake which had been discovered too late for me to be stopped at Kastrup. A message had therefore been transmitted to the Berlin Embassy which had resulted in a disgruntled third secretary being sent from a warm office to a draughty airfield to rectify a mistake that wasn't his. Taking from his overcoat pocket a stamp pad and stamp he proceeded to air his displeasure by stamping indelible mauve cancellation marks across the offending visa in my passport.

With the shock and disappointment seeping into my brain I watched the death of my dream. As it disintegrated into a thousand pieces cold anger filled the vacuum of my heart.

There was murder in my eyes as, still on the well-tried business theme, I loosed a verbal torrent on the head of the wretched little secretary. He stared at me owlishly through thick-lensed spectacles

obviously not understanding a word. Gradually the sense of my outburst was hammered into his brain. His infuriating shrugs only had the
effect of prolonging the hammering and when at last he got in a few
words of his own it didn't help one bit.

"This is not a commercial matter," he explained as if he was dealing
with someone else's child. "That is not my department."

Departments, formalities, entry visas, transit visas, double
transit visas, exit permits, marriage permits. All the ridiculous
machinery of delay and frustration welled up into one big bubble and
burst.

"All you bloody government lackeys are the same," I roared to an
astonished audience. "All locked up tight in your stupid little departments not caring a tuppenny damn what happens so long as your own
fat arses are firmly seated in your departmental chairs!" During my
recital the typewriters had come to a slow standstill and the silence
that followed was as positive as applause.

The English-speaking policeman laid a hand on my arm but I had
shot my bolt. I noticed the typists were enjoying the situation. The
Czech saw it, too, and diplomatically withdrew.

But for me the ordeal was not over. My policeman, obviously an
expert at pouring oil on troubled waters, purred in my ear something
about an aircraft departing for Copenhagen in about two hours. My
journey would be gratis; courtesy of C.S.A.

Swallowing my anger I told him that, with my visit ruined, I would
return to England the direct route from Berlin, thank you.

The police officer avoided my eye. "There is the little matter of
the transit visa," he said quietly as if fearing further storms.

"Yes, but I shall get one in Berlin, or possibly I can—." I was
going to say "fly out" but my reply faded to silence at the realisation
of what the man was trying to tell me.

I started up again: "You mean I've got to fly hundreds of miles in
the wrong direction because I'm not allowed to cross a couple of
miles of the sacred territory of the German Democratic Bloody
Republic!" I spoke my bitter thoughts aloud and the policeman
pretended not to hear.

The flight back to Kastrup was a bad dream. My anger was but a
water-spout in a dead sea of hopelessness. Up to the moment of my
passport being visaed at the Copenhagen Embassy I was prepared for
failure; in fact I had a built-in complex for failure that had been well
nourished over the years but to be rebuffed on the threshold of a hard
earned success was cruelty indeed.

Like the refused visa of my friend this second rebuff would still not greatly affect operation of the "Polish plan". I would just have to get the preliminaries through to Anna by letter using a clumsy code we had evolved between us. The props that reposed in my baggage I would have to take with me to Poland. It would be difficult of course—whoever heard of using a mountain cave as a tailoring and make-up salon!—but then we thrived upon difficulties.

No, it was just the eclipse of another tryst with the girl I loved that hurt the most. At least I could be thankful for not having told Anna of my coming. That way only one heart felt the lash of defeat.

The friendly gaiety of the Danish capital acted as a tonic to my depression. Before I left for home I closed the one last avenue of hope and telephoned my friendly consul general in Oslo.

"He is not available," said a suspicious voice.

Without giving my name I asked about the chances of obtaining a transit visa for Czechoslovakia. Urgent business in the Czech capital and all that.

"Why don't you apply in Copenhagen?"

I was ready for that one. Following my business in Denmark I would have to continue to Norway, and it was from there that I would want to go to Prague.

The voice in Oslo said wait a minute. There was more caution than hesitation provoked by a switch to an unaccustomed language.

"All visa applications must be referred to Prague," said a new voice.

"Even transit visas?"

"All visas?"

I was reluctant to let the voice go. "But you granted me one without difficulty last year."

This time the pause was pregnant.

"You name? Is it not Mr. Portway?" asked the voice thin with suspicion.

I saw no reason to deny the charge. "Yes, but I see no reason—."

A loud click sounded in my ear and I was talking to myself. Metaphorically I chalked a long thin line through Scandinavia.

CHAPTER 15

The Breakthrough

Human reaction to news of great import can form an interesting study. The game of "word association", in which a questioner speaks a word and the subject replies with another; the first to enter his head, gives a revealing, and sometimes amusing insight into one's subconscious.

My reaction to the abruptly announced intention by Fenner Brockway to go to Prague to intercede directly on my behalf was strange indeed. Instead of joy and gratitude that should have been the normal emotion a chary disappointment came over me; a disappointment born of the fact that it might mean the postponement or even shelving of the "Polish plan".

The new year had started on an optimistic note with Fenner Brockway making further representations to the Czech Ambassador in London. I appreciated that my distinguished friend was doing all in his power for me but the diplomatic approach seemed but a dead end. The "Polish plan"—a direct action operation—had firmly rooted itself in my mind and was, to me, the only solution.

A few weeks later, over lunch with him came Fenner Brockway's decision to go to Prague on my behalf. With coffee we discussed dates and details but, such was my inborn pessimism, that it failed to douse my own programme by one iota. Even after the Copenhagen episode my singleness of purpose had narrowed to the problem of sending details of the plan to Anna.

Suddenly from a very different quarter a new development burst upon the scene. My first reaction was plain disbelief. I could easier believe in fairyland. Worn down at last by incessant clamour the Czech authorities had begun, it seemed, the ponderous process of expelling Anna from her homeland......

Eight hundred miles away over on the other side of Europe Anna gazed with wide-eyed incredulity at the typed letter in her hand. It had come that morning from the Ministry of the Interior in Prague. "If she could complete the following formalities," it read in effect, "she would be allowed to leave the country". A list of certificates to be obtained terminated the brief communication.

Hardly daring to believe her senses, Anna went in search of her father for confirmation, support and parental advice. Equally incredulous, he could only offer the sort of advice she did not want to hear, as also did her mother and the other members of the family.

Still in a daze, Anna made tracks for the local solicitor to obtain a more practical opinion. In the cold legal surroundings of his office she obtained the confirmation she needed and set in motion the paper-chase of seven certificates that stood between her and one of the most elusive but sought-after pieces of paper in all Czechoslovakia—an exit permit.

Five exasperating weeks it took to accomplish the task. The National Bank could only issue a nil liability certificate if the State Customs would supply a counter-certificate to the effect that no property was being taken out of the country. The District National Committee (County Council) needed confirmation that she would be in a position to obtain registration as a British subject, but the British Consul was unable to give it since the applicant was not yet in a position to apply. *Cedok* could not supply an air ticket to any Western European destination without payment in sterling or dollars, whilst a train ticket paid for in Czech currency could only be made valid to the border. In turn the German, French, Belgium and Dutch Consulates were unable to consider the granting of even a transit visa within a period of two months and, since the applicant was technically stateless would probably end up in a displaced persons' camp anyway.

By the end of the first month Anna had scored a total of four certificates but some of these were threatening to expire. Fast coming to the conclusion that the Authorities were playing a cruel game of cat-and-mouse she all but gave it up when, abruptly tiring of the sport, the Ministry of the Interior produced the master-key certificate that fitted the locks of the remainder. This was a statement irrecoverably divesting her of Czech nationality.

Stateless, penniless, propertyless and jobless, the State could find no reason for keeping her. But because, being stateless, she could hold no passport, how could an exit visa be furnished? To overcome the problem of its own making the Ministry had but two alternatives. One was to pass a new law and the other to issue a stateless person's travel document not legally recognised by all countries in Europe. They chose the easy way and made up a travel document to which to affix the necessary seals and stamps of an exit visa. As long as she could leave the country who were they to bother about the consequences?

Possessed of an air ticket sent by me, and very little else Anna took leave of her family. The kitchen-living room, which for so long had been the venue of my dream of reunion, became the stage for the final parting. And the silent tears shed were of both joy and sadness.

On Sunday, the seventeenth of March, at Ruzyne Airport Anna boarded an Air-France Viscount for a one-way flight to Paris.

The first news of her impending release came from Anna and I could scarcely believe the words I was reading. That it was a trick was wholly certain and I clung for my sanity to the rock that was our "Polish plan".

A telegram from the House of Commons followed. It read "Permit granted conditional renounce Czech nationality" and was signed "Fenner Brockway". One person believed it anyway.

The days that followed brought further missives that confirmed and reconfirmed the good intentions of some bureaucratic stronghold in Prague. Gradually I loosened my hold on the "plan".

Thereafter I lived in a fever of mounting excitement and if a day passed without a telegram or letter from Anna my confused mind inflated it into a major disaster until the subsequent communication released the pressure. From not only Anna did they come. Cold factual epistles from the Foreign Office couching their joyous tidings in grey formal words, screeds from the Committee of Human Rights presenting in the chatty American style the likelihood of a happy ending to United Nations intervention, a note from Mr. R. A. Butler, now Chancellor of the Exchequer, confirming all that was already being confirmed, and even a request from Independent Television to cover the wedding! Everyone wanted to be on the bandwagon.

Finally came the telegram for which I was waiting. Sent by Anna it announced simply "Arriving Orly Sunday Seventeenth Twenty Twenty". The flimsy paper spun crazily and I closed my eyes as a great shudder passed through me. I came out the other side into the peace of undiluted happiness.

On Saturday, the sixteenth of March, I boarded the "Golden Arrow" night express to Paris.

The French capital lay under a damp blanket of sky. In the Champs Elysees the leafless trees alone showed mute promise of a spring that a chill wind did its best to destroy.

Hands deep in my pockets I strolled towards the Etoile. Where I was going I had no particular idea. Simply to pass the time was all that mattered. Not until twenty minutes past eight that night would I be able to keep the final tryst which would end the five years of waiting, scheming, planning and frustration that had become my life.

Sleep had been impossible on the train ferry. At the Gare St. Lazare I had checked the time of the departure, together with the sleeper reservation, of the London-bound train some thirty-six hours hence, basking in the knowledge that there would be two of us for the journey home.

From the station I had made my way to the Madeleine and a luxury hotel where rooms had been booked in readiness. Washed and shaved and a second very *"petit dejeuner"* stowed away I stretched out untidily on the bed pretending to relax.

As with pictures in the fire the intricate pattern of the ceiling made a screen for the utterances of my wild thoughts there to be enacted, again and again, the imagined drama of Anna's arrival at the airport. The roar of traffic outside the hotel became the scream of a turbo-jet, the chatter of voices in the passage the loudspeaker announcement of her flight's arrival. And the pattern faded to give way for the small figure as she detached herself from the group walking from the aircraft. A moment later she was in my arms hugging me close to her. I lay there feeling the quiver of her body and, as I smelt the perfume of her hair, my heart exploded in a burst of joy.

The picture faded as my mind wandered into the delicious problems of a short week-end in Paris. Anna would be tired; possibly confused. So we would have an intimate little meal together in one of the expensive restaurants on the Boulevard Haussman close by the hotel. Afterwards, perhaps a short stroll window-gazing into shops the like of which she would have never seen before. Next day we would sleep late prior to a morning tour of the French capital. I would show her the glories of the Notre Dame, the Sacre-Coeur and the Arc de Triomphe. We would stroll arm in arm along the banks of the Seine to the Louvre, the Tuileries and the white-stoned Palais de Chaillot. We would look down upon the magnificence of the city from the summit of the Eiffel Tower and, having generated a healthy appetite, descend to lower altitudes for an aperitif and lunch in the Montmartre district. My mind laboured on......

Impatience intruded and I found myself looking at the patterns on the ceiling again and they were just patterns. I rose and left the hotel. But the distractions of the Paris streets gave me no peace. I treated myself to a mediocre lunch and lost two hours in the stale warmth of a cinema trying to make sense of an American psychological thriller which would probably have been incomprehensible even if it had been in English. Fully half an hour before I intended I found myself approaching the air terminal in the Place d'Invalides.

Here at least I could watch other people fall slaves to the clock and from my own lofty pinnacle of experience gain cynical amusement from their discomfort. The panic over the inaudible announcements, the worried arguments about flight schedules, the general fingernail-biting brinkmanship of an airport terminal full of week-end travellers.

With an hour to go before my coach left for Orly to connect with the incoming Viscount from Prague I gazed upon the pattern of faces ever-changing as in a kaleidoscope. Puzzled faces, frustrated faces, angry faces, determined faces, "know it all" and "done it before" faces. They all told a story and I wondered idly what my own revealed. From faces I turned to the advertisements. Bosoms and booze was the monotonous theme. One could justifiably accuse the French of having two-track minds. I smiled to myself as my eyes stole back to the clock.

The crisp, precise tones announcing the flight number served by my coach still managed to take me by surprise. In a trio of languages the instruction was repeated and the announcer was struggling through a spasm of gallic German when I took my seat.

Sweeping through the southern environs of the city on to the Fontainebleau road and past the enormous *Gaz de France* industrial complex the myriad lights grew dimmer. Thirty-five minutes dead after leaving the Invalides the coach pulled into the massive concrete arrival bay of Orly Airport.

In the crowded lounge I stalked up and down unable to find the patience to sit. My usual cloud of eleventh-hour doubts had arisen and I battled with morbid thoughts as I waited for the arrival of the flight from Prague. Would she be aboard the aircraft? Could anything have gone wrong in Prague? I conjured up a list of possible eventualities that might have prevented her departure. Depressed beyond measure I gave intense attention to a flight time-table to Bangkok.

"Air France announce the arrival of…", even had the announcement been in Siamese, its meaning would have been crystal clear. My heart performed a somersault and beat madly at my ribs. I strained my ears for the sound of aero engines, my eyes rivetted on to the door through which the arrivals had to pass. A slight hush fell on the community and I realised that others, besides myself, were committed to a reunion.

The double doors at one end of the lounge were thrown open by an official. The waiting throng tensed and those with relatives and friends to meet crowded to the rope barrier. Other announcements of departures went unheard as dozens of eyes spotlighted a doorway that had become the wings of a stage. Minutes, the length of hours, ticked by.

Without warning the first actor made his bow. A small man in an overcoat too big for him stood blinking in the neon light. He grappled with stage-fright as his eyes took in his unexpected audience and, self-consciously shrinking into his coat like a tortoise, scuttled out of sight and mind. Next a middle-aged couple stood bewildered in the tense unsmiling stare but were saved by a reaction from the stalls. A cry of welcome softened the silence and their ordeal was over. They too passed into the wings and were gone. A young woman, unmistakably French, held the stage and her own before being claimed. Her doting parents, from the body of the audience, ushered her chatteringly into oblivion. So it went on and the audience shrank until I stood amongst a little group that had themselves become the actors.

With the group down to three I was in a state of near-panic. A fat woman fell into the arms of a worried hubby and we were two. My companion fitted a newly-fledged schoolmaster taking life very seriously indeed. He smiled severely at me as understanding passed between us but any closer ties that might have bound us were flung aside as he tripped forward to meet his wayward charge. I was alone.

With the slamming shut of the door my hopes dived to rock bottom. What could have happened? What perverted authority could sink to such abysmal depths? A fierce anger stirred again within me. I strode up to the door and hammered on its blank indifferent surface. A customs man opened it to stare at me with an expression similar to that of the door. I opened my mouth to demand confirmation that all passengers were accounted for on the Prague flight but not a word passed my lips. In speechless wonderment I beheld Anna arguing in fluent French with a gesticulating official.

She was over the other side of the customs hall but I could hear her voice raised in bewildered indignation. For a moment I allowed a warm torrent of relief to flow over me before stepping forward to be held back by the guardian of the door.

"She's my fiancee," I said as if it gave me the right to the whole airport. I brushed the man's arm aside but he stood his ground.

I tried again. "Why is my fiancee being held?" My voice was sullen with anger.

"You are English?"

I failed to see what it had to do with it but replied that I was.

"Just a moment, please." The customs man walked over to Anna's inquisitor and said something to him. Anna understood what he said and looked round for me. I saw the baffled expression on her face give way to a fleeting smile of joy.

Another man joined the little group and made a great show of examining Anna's papers. It was he who came over to me to offer explanations.

He spoke perfect English in a soft competent manner. "I'm afraid that this lady has not a proper passport," he explained. His next words exploded like a bomb in my ears. **" I regret she will have to return to Prague."**

I said nothing for the simple reason that I was speechless. Instead I walked firmly over to Anna. Tightly holding hands we faced the inquisition together.

"What's wrong with her passport?" I demanded.

The senior official explained that Anna's travel papers in no way constituted a passport. Neither had she a French visa.

My retort was that, being stateless, she could not hold a proper passport. And that she did have a British visa.

The official admitted that she had. But this was France, and...

"Well, why not put her on the next aeroplane to England. Why send her back when, with no more trouble, you can send her forward." I interrupted the man's futile objections. The gist of the conversation was threatening to be painfully similar to others I could remember. But this one was occurring in France, the free West. I felt a flush of shame.

Driven on by the sting I continued my thrust. I wasn't angry anymore; just incredulous. Five years we had been fighting the whole Cominform to see one another and to become man and wife. Now, on the very threshold of victory a Frenchman, a citizen of a country in which love and romance were on a par with the Marseillaise, wanted to destroy everything because the right words were not on a piece of paper. I demanded time to contact the Chancellor of the Exchequer in London, the Foreign Minister, the Prime Minister, the United Nations. Even the—

The official saw I meant business. He hesitated and was lost.

"I will make further investigations," he promised in a kindlier tone and I knew he was in retreat.

131

I turned to Anna and met her gaze. There were tears in the big turquoise eyes. My heart turned another somersault and threatened to choke me.

"Hello," I said weakly. And there in the immigration building of Orly Airport I took my fiancee tenderly into a great bear-hug. My mouth found her cool parted lips.

At least one little piece of the dream was coming true.

We spent the night sharing a hard leather armchair in the detention room. It was not a comfortable night and the surroundings were a far cry from those envisaged in my programme. But we were together and that was enough. We got no sleep but the comings and goings of an assortment of immigration officials became not so unwelcome as the decision to allow Anna to proceed to London was made.

No, she could not leave the airport. She would be put aboard the early-morning service to Heathrow. Yes, she must have a ticket. I could go with her if I too could get a ticket, and there was a seat to spare. I looked mournfully at Anna's and my useless train tickets and sleeper reservation vouchers. Would Air-France consider... no, they would not. The first coach back to the terminal left Orly about four in the morning. I would be able to apply for the air tickets then.

The details suddenly didn't seem important any more. A wave of fatigue engulfed me. But Anna's head was on my shoulder and the smell of her hair was in my nostrils. The ordeal of five years was sliding away from us. I was very very happy.

Darkness still gripped the city as I returned in a near empty coach to the Invalides. The streets of Paris were strangely silent as if a plague had struck down its noisy throngs. Wreaths of mist clung to the dying night.

Back in the air terminal I shook two single tickets for the off-peak flight to London out of a sleepy-eyed clerk. Take-off was at six-thirty and the coach that served the flight left an hour earlier.

I consulted my watch and estimated a bare fifty five minutes to reach my hotel, re-pack, settle an unprofitable account, and return.

Only the pigeons, a few street cleaners and a curious gendarme observed my dash across the impressive void of the Place de la Concorde, and on past the pillared bulk of the Madeleine into the Boulevard Haussman. A tiresome night porter at the hotel had some objections to settling an account at so early an hour, but upon being told it was now or never grumpily made it now.

I swung through the glass doors of the terminal, even with the added impediment of a suitcase, with four minutes to spare. Staggering into the waiting coach I collapsed into a corner seat. Daylight gave me opportunity to see more of the familiar route to Orly but the magic of Paris had lost its kick. All I could see was a vision of a girl tired, bewildered and trusting, anxiously awaiting my return in a bleak detention room.

I found her there amidst the clamour of an airport awakening. Arm in arm we joined the short queue for customs clearance. As we walked across the concrete apron towards the stationary Viscount, a pale sun broke through the dispersing clouds of night, offering promise of a fine day ahead.

For the two of us the years of twilight were over.

CHAPTER 16

Bitter Victory

On the fifth day of April 1957 we were married in St. Mary's Church, Ilford under the glare of press and television publicity and, following an idyllic honeymoon in Ireland, set up home near Gosfield in Essex. In course of time we produced a daughter and a son and our happiness was complete.

Thus the answer to the question "How did you meet your wife?" is likewise complete and the story that has provided the answer has, like in the fairy tales of old, a happy ending. But we live in the second half of the twentieth century and straightforward happy endings to stories are no longer the vogue. There has to be a sting in the tail; a double exit, call it what you like. This story also follows the pattern of the new convention and fact likewise seemed to find the fairy-tale finish too corny an ending. The clouds in the sky at last wore a silver lining but they also obscured a scudding maelstrom in their wake.

So, not quite, is it the end of the story.

For a number of years Anna and I were pointedly persona non grata in Czechoslovakia. At first we accepted this as small price to pay for the prize our combined perseverance had won for us. But Anna's parents, in the evening of their lives, loudly voiced a natural desire to see both us and their new grandchildren. It was a voice we could not ignore and, with Anna now a British subject, we occasionally succeeded in beating the ban using ruses somewhat reminiscent of earlier days.

It was during such rare visits that we confirmed an ugly portend that had not become manifest in the censored letters that reached us in Britain. The fact that Anna had left her country in a legally constituted manner had not prevented the State from taking an undramatic but callous revenge on those she left behind.

Outwardly the situation in the subject countries of Eastern Europe showed a steady improvement. Tourists were encouraged to see the beauty of Prague and the quiet loveliness of the countryside. Trade blossomed when it suited the economy and by the mid-1960's the heavy hand of Stalinism had turned to a subtly restraining touch. But freedom still could raise no voice in Czechoslovakia even if its chains had been sheathed in nylon. Neither had its warders forgotten or forgiven the episode of Anna's denunciation of the Communist creed and had turned their nasty attentions on to the remaining members of the family. They knew that the two parents were aged and past caring; also that the elder daughter had a useful job on the railways and therefore was remunerative to the State. But the youngest daughter Marie and her husband Pavel were fair game. Hadn't he already served a term of imprisonment for an attempted escape and weren't they both known sympathisers of the West? The carrot of emigration papers had already been dangled before them. A little job of simple espionage in Scandinavia was the deal. But the fool had rebuffed it. Yes, that was where a little quiet revenge would hurt most.

The fact that Pavel held a degree in electronics at the University of Prague mattered not at all. The job that such a degree would normally carry could not be undertaken by so politically unreliable a craftsman. He wasn't even a member of the Party. So Pavel found work where he could, in factories and in coal-mines, while the electronics were left in the clumsy hands of more "reliable", if less intelligent, folk. It was jobs for the boys with a vengeance. By simple ability Pavel frequently rose above the level of his workmates and was recommended for promotion. But promotion entailed the checking of the files and straightaway his pedestal of accomplishment was kicked from under him. Neither did the other members of the family get off scott-free. Anna's father was regularly called to the local S.T.B. Office for "discussion" and Milena, the eldest daughter, was barred from works visits abroad. Pinpricks for sure but pinpricks can hurt.

By 1965 little tit-bits of freedom were being magnanimously thrown to the masses. Fragments of free opinion were appearing in certain journals, celluloid epics from Britain, France and America were being tolerated to appease an appetite for knowledge of the Western World. One member per family at a time was even allowed to visit relatives abroad. These and other crumbs were hungrily devoured but, instead of getting indigestion, the masses wanted more.

It was in 1965, as the rumblings of discontent were increasing in a country that was beginning to realise at last how far it had been taken for a ride, that Pavel decided he had had enough.

More carefully watched than most of his compatriots he saw no hope of putting into practice any of the grandiose schemes of escape he and I had often discussed. Moreover he had the handicap of a wife.

It was no good planning anything. The frontiers were death traps and his legal chances nil. Even flying out by aero club aircraft (Pavel held a pilot's licence) was a hopeless endeavour for MIG jet fighters had orders to shoot down without mercy any such machines that strayed within 25 miles of the borders. He would simply have to await an opportunity when his watchers dropped their guard.

Seldom however was the S.T.B. careless in the execution of its task. In fact, as far as Pavel was concerned, it had happened only once in seventeen years.

But it was once too often.

CHAPTER 17

Rijeka Rendezvous

We met, Pavel and I, on the sun terrace of the Hotel Kontinental, Rijeka, that sundrenched afternoon of 23rd July. Around us the Yugoslav seaport shone a bleached white against the blue of the Adriatic. The warmth of Pavel's handshake spoke more eloquently than his limited English of his pleasure—and relief—at seeing me. An exchange of telegrams had brought me a thousand miles from England and him more than half that distance from Czechoslovakia. For Pavel the journey was to shape the destiny of his life and I was one of the props. A vital prop. He said he knew I'd come, his bronzed lean face wreathed in smiles. But the relief was there all the same.

The ways of Communist minds are strange. With all their back-biting tactics against Anna's family they occasionally allowed Marie a brief visit to England. More often than not her application was refused but once in a while the ban was lifted. Pavel, of course, had to remain behind, a living guarantee that she would return. Yet within these few short weeks which his government irregularly allowed Marie beyond the gates Pavel knew to be his only chance for both of them to discard the yoke of oppression. He turned his eyes southwards to neighbouring Hungary and, beyond, Yugoslavia. There lay a fellow Socialist Republic of a lesser shade of red and, more important, possessing a common and less lethal border with the West.

At first he could not synchronise his own and Marie's movements. Either Marie was refused a passport with which to visit England or Pavel's application to visit Yugoslavia was delayed until her safe return. In 1967 restrictions on travel within the Eastern bloc were eased still further and, as a gesture to International Tourist Year, Yugoslavia had temporarily dispensed with the necessity of entry visas. In June Marie was granted permission to visit England. With this combination Pavel was quick to realise the long awaited opportunity to be within his grasp.

Marie left for London in July and Pavel quietly put in hand arrangements to visit Yugoslavia ostensibly for a camping holiday. Using a companion to make the necessary application for a foreign currency allowance he avoided the attention of State Security. The rest was easy. Knowing that the transit visa for Hungary, athwart the route to Yugoslavia, could be obtained without reference to Czech authority, Pavel marshalled his aces.

In the middle of the night, driving the little Volkswagen that was his pride and joy Pavel and his trusted companion left travelling south. Of his secret intentions they told no-one. Already he had paid for one attempt to turn the dream of freedom into reality with the nightmare of eighteen months imprisonment. It could equally apply to those who helped or who even had knowledge of or acquiesced in the plot. This time the trick simply **had** to work.

We left Rijeka together and threading our way in the little car past the hulks of half completed ships cradled by slender cranes, ascended the wooded heights behind the town. Pavel's companion would return to Czechoslovakia alone by train there, in due course, to report the defection. That way nobody would get hurt. The heat of the sun was beginning to die and we had two hours in which to reach a dot on my map that, seventy kilometres away, I had designated to be Pavel's crossing point into Italy.

The day before in a hired car with Tony, a Maltese friend who spoke Italian, I had reconnoitred the tongue of Italian territory protruding into Yugoslavia behind Trieste. And, so doing, had come across Monrupino. From the church that perched atop of the dramatic little hill the border looked unguarded, unwatched, tranquil. Shimmering in the midday sun the valley was just one of many, parched and scorched, that slept to the twittering lullaby of crickets. An Italian peasant, seeing our interest, pointed out the line of the frontier curving along the middle of the valley. Hidden amongst the trees and scrub we picked out a watch-tower near a road and another on the brow of a hill. There were no minefields or wire-fences he said but—. He gave us a shrewd look half-guessing the reason for our interest, "but there are many soldiers with, what you call, automatic guns. They are bad shots but—." In Italian "but" is a most eloquent word. Fill the air with lead, we supposed, and something was likely to get hit.

Defying the butterflies in my stomach Tony and I made our plans. With him watching from this most perfect observation point I would, from the Yugoslav side, accompany Pavel to within twenty yards of the border, create a diversion, and the job would be done. I would return to Pavel's car and, alone, make my way back via the main checkpoint at Sezana to Trieste. With the "Open Sesame" of a British passport I would invoke no questions. Tony would collect Pavel on the Italian side of the border and likewise return to Trieste. Operations would commence at ten o'clock tomorrow night as the

138

sun sunk below Monrupino church. I had quite a job to dissuade the determined Tony from a plan to open up with an old Colt revolver to give covering fire at the appropriate moment. After all we didn't want to start a war. Look what happened down the road at Sarajevo...

The location of Vogliano, the tiny hamlet close to the border on the Yugoslav side that Tony and I had pinpointed as the base for our operation, was by no means easy to find. Pavel and I were coming up to it from behind now and my Italian Touring Club map was both out of date and inaccurate. Furthermore an optimistic cartographer had insisted upon using the original Italian place-names for the Istran peninsula and the area ceded to the Yugoslavs in 1947.

It was the local checkpoint—the one Tony and I had seen earlier—we found first. Hastily we reversed, turned and drove watchfully back to the cluster of houses that had hidden the junction to Vogliano.

We left the car beneath a tree in a strategic position for a quick getaway. Vogliano was indicated as 1 Kilometre, the route being no more than a cart track. Taking advantage of the remaining daylight we decided upon an open reconnaissance of the area, locating a good well-sheltered section of the border where we would hide up until dusk or darkness. The track ran westwards, roughly parallel with the border. On our left, the silhouette of Monrupino church stood out starkly on its mound against a blood-red sunset. Somewhere up there amid the granite walls Tony would be watching and waiting.

Abruptly we were in the village. But something was different about the small cluster of houses that hemmed us in. The place was not dead like other frontier villages I remembered though the street was empty. I felt the eyes of hidden citizens upon us from behind half drawn lace curtains. An old man, sucking an ancient pipe, surveyed us morosely from a doorway. A lame dog skulked by to turn and bark defiance—the only noise in a community of silence.

Round a corner the road was barred by a striped barrier pole. We sheered away from it and took another track leading away from the border.

A shout brought us to a halt. A policeman, buckling on a pistol belt, emerged from a house. He asked us where we were going. Ready with our cover stories I explained in a mixture of English, Italian and German that we had been with the Yugoslav partisans here during the war and had returned to the scene. With Tony I had previously tried it on the Italians who had been suitably impressed but the policeman, even when Pavel had clarified my explanations and added a few of his own, was not so gullible. He shrugged disinterestedly, examined our passports and told us we were in a forbidden zone and must leave immediately. Hastily we retreated.

Halfway back along the track, out of sight of the village, we slipped into an orchard with the intention of concealing ourselves until nightfall. We lay sprawled out behind a hedge still acting the part of unconcerned tourists though our intentions were hardening. A little more dusk and we would become animals of the night. The demarcation line of the frontier was but a hundred yards to our front. Some scrubby bushes provided isolated stepping-stones of cover but only darkness could screen the open ground between. The watchtower was more than a quarter of a mile to the left. At that range I doubted if a searchlight would be effective.

Impatient to get the job done we started to move forward using the last hour of daylight to find a spring board in the middle of no-man's land. With great stealth we slithered on our stomachs over the prickly stubble. But we had not allowed for the craftiness of the policeman. His suspicions aroused by Pavel's Czech travel document he had silently followed us. Now he emerged to stand over us, a hand resting warily on his pistol butt.

We had fewer explanations this time. Caught with our pants down we could only feel like naughty schoolboys and hope that we would be treated as such. I did mumble something about looking for birds nests but, perhaps fortunately, the man failed to understand. Anyway it was the wrong season. Curtly he ordered us to follow him and conversation died as the three of us walked to where we had left the car. Passing by, and pretending it wasn't ours, we tramped another mile to the checkpoint.

In the office of the customs house we were questioned in turn, our replies presumably being compared. A number of telephone calls of considerable duration were made. Our partisan stories caused flickers of interest, but also aroused some close questioning on the pertinent details. This was tricky for I had learnt of rival factions in the partisan district of Slovenia, and hard feelings still lingered on whenever the spiky subject of Trieste was involved. Everything we said was thumped out for posterity on an antiquated typewriter and I was halfway through a complicated rigmarole about the confounded partisans; desperately playing it neutral, when this line of interrogation came to an abrupt halt as did a home-going Italian who, dazed by a surfeit of slivovice, ran his motorcycle full-tilt into the lowered frontier pole!

We all ran into the road to pick up the pieces and straighten the bent pole. The casualty was treated to a strong slug of cognac even though, to my unmedical mind, it seemed a case of coals to Newcastle. Pavel and I, back in the guardhouse, intimated that we were thirsty but all we rated was a glass of ersatz fruit squash.

The hours passed and the only information I could get out of any of the various policemen who came on and off duty was that we were awaiting the arrival of a more senior police officer. The night blotted out the tantalising view of Monrupino and I thought of the unfortunate Tony patiently waiting. Lines of young soldiers bristling with automatic weapons and accompanied by hungry-looking Alsation dogs spewed from a small barracks opposite to disappear into the undergrowth. Pavel and I watched them go in silent trepidation. We wondered if they were all such bad shots...

I still had one card up my sleeve, or, to be exact, in my wallet. As we waited anxiously for developments I felt it burning a hole in my pocket. Some weeks earlier I had again lunched with Fenner Brockway, then a Life Peer. Beyond the fact that my brother-in-law was likely to want to emigrate westwards from Yugoslavia I told him nothing of my own possible involvement in an illegal operation. Indeed the good man didn't want to know for while he could truthfully profess ignorance of any intended "crime" he could help us by supplying me with letters requesting "help for the bearer" to the British Consular authorities in Italy as well as the Government of Yugoslavia. It was this Yugoslav letter that now gave rise to my concern. On crested notepaper it asked full facilities "without let or hindrance" of none other than his friend President Tito!

It only needed the most perfunctory of searches for the letter to come to light. And at this stage of the proceedings it could but cause us acute embarrassment. I felt reasonably confident of being able to talk ourselves out of our present predicament but disclosure of the contents of the letter would be tantamount to an admission of guilt. Only if Pavel was threatened with deportation to his own country would I invoke the President and, if necessary, his whole Cabinet.

It was well past midnight when a police captain arrived at the checkpoint. An unfriendly individual, he gruffly indicated that we were to be taken to the local headquarters at Cezana. Seeing no point in continuing the pretence of having no car we asked if we could take the Volkswagen. Nobody showed any surprise at the disclosure and, accompanied by an escort of five policemen, we were given a lift in the police jeep back to the Vogliano junction. Distributing the load in the two cars we were directed along the roughest of tracks that Tony and I had earlier written off, from its other end, as impassable.

Pavel drove and I sat beside him with two policemen breathing garlic down our necks.

In the main square of the township of Cezana we were taken into a barrack-like building that appeared to serve as police station, jail, council chamber, kindergarten and cats home. In the charge room another officer bade us a friendly welcome and put us through a mild interrogation. We stuck to our partisan routine but I had decided the time had come for a counter attack. I thought I knew too where I could touch on a raw spot. Accordingly while the officer was grappling with his typewriter (why, oh, why cannot police forces the world over master the simple art of typing?!) I politely but firmly demanded to know what crime we had committed beyond an ignorance of the border regulations and that, if they wished to hold us longer, I should require, by international law, to see my Consul— There was one in Lujubjana, I'd checked. Finally I hinted that if these conditions weren't met I'd make such a hell of a noise about it no British tourist would come near Yugoslavia for years.

Results were sensational. The officer visibly winced, pressed two keys at the same time and became even more friendly than before. He shrugged his shoulders resignedly, offered us cigarettes; then rushed into the adjoining telephone exchange. We heard him shouting even through the thick stone walls.

He returned beaming and gave us a light-hearted lecture on border zone regulations. Handing back our passports he distributed hand-shakes and we were free.

Amazed, I followed Pavel into the street. Not for a moment did I expect this turn of events. At the best could I visualize my own release but Pavel was a foreigner without even the ''protection'' of a sterling potential. But it was not for me to reason why and we quickly evapor-ated into the narrow silent streets of the town.

Congratulating ourselves on our luck it came to us that we were after all, only back where we started from. A kind of ''Dunkirk'' in fact. We had been delivered from a disaster but hardly had we scored a victory. Our tired minds refused to register on what the next move was to be. Better to sleep on it.

I left Pavel at the annexe of a local hotel and, taking his car, arranged to return in the morning. For me it was the bright lights of Trieste again to mitigate the disappointment. The frontier was but a mile and a half down the road and to my intense surprise the border people—Italian as well as Yugoslav—were not the slightest bit interested in the Czech-registered car. But later Tony was—he had a seventeen-kilometre walk.

CHAPTER 18

The Pregnant Unicorn

It was hardly worth returning to Trieste. Within very few hours I was back in Cezana there to collect Pavel and, together, drive into the wilderness.

Together too, we gazed across the vast expanse of tree-shrouded hills, our eyes roving up and over the double crest. My heart sank at the formidable task that I had set my brother-in-law. He himself was plainly aghast. The early afternoon sun beat down with cruel intensity —an added challenge to the unknown hazards of the frontier that ran along the reverse slope of the second crest.

I had chosen the place after a long study of the map. Well wooded hills way off the beaten track seemed to offer the best way out. With a troubled heart and a powerful longing to accompany him, I left Pavel on a forgotten dust road somewhere between the hamlets of Vallegrande and Pliscovizza di Madonna. But it was essentially a one-man job. Tony and I would meet him in the Italian village of Sgonico on the other side. We would wait all night if necessary. Pavel hated my leaving, and I hated myself for the brutal way I was pushing him into hideous danger. But it had to be done. Either that or surrender. In the driving mirror I watched him, a sad forlorn figure, swallowed up in a cloud of dust.

Again I crossed over into Italian territory to join Tony impatiently awaiting my return. Driving at breakneck speed along the little roads that criss-cross the plateau above Trieste we found Sgonico and established our headquarters under the vine-sheltered portico of the local *albergo*. There was absolutely no need for haste since we had many hours to kill but poor Tony's role in the operation was a waiting one and he craved a little action. Now, as we sipped cold lager, I was to share his role. The experience made an immediate impact that seared my soul. Had I sent a man to savage captivity or even death? Had I failed his wife who waited? Had I failed my own whose faith I bore? And fear grew in the fertile abyss of my torment.

In the late afternoon, in spite of the intense heat, I skulked deep into the border zone passing the warning notices that sprinkled the summits of the hills behind the village. The urge to share Pavel's burden of danger stirred restlessly within me.

Sgonico was a village that was more Serb than Italian. Near the dilapidated church a war memorial in the heroic style beloved by Communism listed names that were certainly not of Italian stock. Many, no doubt, had died fighting a vanquished enemy who had finally won the village off the battlefield. There was an irony in the situation that showed in the attitude of its swarthy citizens. In conversation with the clients of the *albergo* Tony and I learnt of conflicting loyalties and divided passions. Devout Catholic, hot-head Communist, pro-Italian, pro-Yugoslav. Religion, politics and nationalism were the life-blood of Sgonico.

Our long sojourn in the village became a subject of curiosity. Treated with friendliness and civility, frequently invited to share a flask of wine, we were nevertheless under increasing suspicion. I wanted to tell the good people of the reason of our visit but whose side were they on?

The storm broke with terrifying abruptness. Tony and I finished our umpteenth beer and watched the lightning lash the bleached roofs and walls of Sgonico with vivid hate. Thunder rolled and a jet black sky prematurely turned day into night. No rain came to Sgonico, but we could hear its angry hiss as it fell on the trees in the hills.

When the tempest had passed the night remained and in the cool fresh darkness I walked into the wet countryside calling Pavel's name in forlorn hope that it would be a beacon for his lost footsteps. Again and again I repeated the manoeuvre but the steaming hills only mocked me with an echo.

Long after midnight we waited even optimistically telephoning our hotel in case of a miracle. But no bedraggled stranger had put in an appearance. Only when the *albergo* wanted to close its doors did we depart with a terrible dread in our hearts. Miracles were not for us this night.

A mile and a whole world north of Sgonico Pavel moved forward again. Through the intense heat of the afternoon and on into the refuge of the evening he had made purposefully slow progress but still he was drenched in sweat. It had run down to sting his eyes and he felt more rivulets coursing down his chest and back to saturate his clothes. He longed to find a sheltered spot to lie down and taste the acrid bliss of a cigarette but the brow of the first crest beckoned him onward. Struggling through the dense undergrowth the second crest made even greater demands and, as the dusk enveloped him in an ever deepening

144

hue, it became increasingly difficult to maintain direction. Only when he neared the summit did he allow himself the luxury of a rest to prepare for the final thrust. For two hours he had relaxed as well as he could content in the knowledge that the border ran along the skyline in sight through the trees. From his bed of dry pine-needles he had listened for the sounds of danger and waited for nightfall. In the silence the emotion of loneliness was greater than that of fear.

Stepping carefully; trying to avoid the snapping of twigs that sounded like fire-crackers in the stillness of the night, Pavel suddenly was no longer alone. Other men were close by. And dogs. He heard the rustle of their movements, the whisper of voices, and once, a low whistle as of a master to his canine charge. His eyes, accustomed to the darkness, picked out a telephone cable, which he followed. A foolish action for it led him only into deeper danger. Crawling, Pavel slid past the reclining figures of uniformed men, their accoutrements and weapons strapped about them. In the very midst of peril he watched with terrified fascination an Alsation dog jump to its feet and sniff the air.

The storm hit them with no warning. For Pavel all sounds and shadows were obliterated by the deluge. Lightning flashes turned the night into vivid shafts of purple fire that threw the silent tree trunks into startling relief. Just for one instant did the yelp of a dog reach through the fury.

He lay flat on the ground as still as the trees. The display of brilliance could work two ways. See and be seen. That he had walked into a patrol was only too evident. That they had failed to spot him was simply luck. For Pavel the storm was not only an offer of protection but a warning. To ignore it would be madness. He would tempt providence no further. Soaked to the skin, the rain hissing round him, he slunk back from whence he came.

The telegram that reached my Trieste hotel next morning lifted a great weight off my mind. I rushed into Tony's bedroom waving the buff paper as if it were a flag of triumph. At least Pavel was alive and at liberty. But we were no further forward than we had been at the start. Pavel was not free. The direct assault on the border was paying no dividends. A more subtle method would have to be employed.

It was Tony who came up with the brainwave. Good old Tony whose waiting and watching brief had seemed so unrewarding. But it had given him time to think. We had already discarded the concealment-in-the-car idea. The odds were too high. And we could all go down, car included. But a "doctored" passport? That was a different matter. Furthermore we had the means.

When I had packed my bag prior to leaving England I had, as an afterthought, included my three cancelled passports. Pavel too had contributed by giving me various articles of personal value, the inference being that I was the lesser insurance risk. These included a spare identity photograph. In addition we could find between us a ballpoint pen, a penknife and, from a nearby stationer's shop, a pot of paste. Finally we had Tony's talent.

With the cheap ballpoint pen and one of my extinct passport photographs he went to work carefully pressing the indented Foreign Office stamp into the back of Pavel's photograph. We had selected the old photograph for its size of stamp, choosing one that fitted nearest into that portion of stamp remaining in the page of my valid passport. Slowly the indentation of part of the Foreign Office cypher appeared on the glossy face of Pavel's photograph. One slip of the pen, a little too much pressure and the masterpiece of forgery would be ruined. But as the scorching sun proclaimed mid-morning Tony produced a small miracle in the bedroom of that sleazy Trieste hotel. With the limited quantity of tools at his disposal the result was, perhaps, not absolute perfection, but under perfunctory inspection and artificial light it would fool anyone. Close scrutiny of that portion of the indented stamp that was on the photograph could produce criticism perhaps. But would a Yugoslav object to an obviously pregnant unicorn?

Next we cut out one of the "Description—Signalement" slips in an old passport and made a few alterations to the entries. Pavel's features were not so very unlike mine so the alterations were kept to a minimum.

We were now ready to transfer the doctored photograph and identity slip to my valid passport but first it was necessary to put Pavel into the picture—literally!

By midday we were back at the Cezana crossing point. Leaving Tony and the car I walked into Yugoslavia using my, as yet, unblemished passport. As usual it was given a glance and stamped by the Yugoslav officials. I had been through the formalities so many times that I knew the drill by heart. When I went out again it would be more carefully examined but not stamped. At night the examination would be more thorough probably because the traffic was less dense and the officials had time to spare. It would therefore be important to choose, as "zero hour", a time when dusk had fallen but traffic not too scarce. I walked the mile and a half to Pavel's hotel where his telegram had indicated I should find him. Over lunch at a terrace table, as far as possible out of earshot of other diners, I outlined the plan to him. He fell in at once with the idea. We decided upon ten o'clock that night as "zero hour" but to delay driving up to the check point until two or more cars had formed a queue. This way he would have a chance to look before he leapt.

I returned the way I came. The Italian officials simply glanced at passports in both directions taking little apparent interest in the comings and goings of a tourist horde. They did however take the registration numbers of cars and ask for insurance papers.

Rejoining Tony we spent a profitable half hour substituting Pavel's photograph for mine and lightly pasting the "new" identity slip over the one in my valid passport. Tidying up the substitution with a pocket knife, india rubber and a dab of petrol we gazed, slightly dubiously, at our handiwork. Under the bright sun it looked an amateurish botched-up sort of job. But it would have to do. Both of us had run out of ideas. Physical and mental exhaustion was beginning to tell and we were snapping at each other like fractious children. Now to get the thing to Pavel.

Hiding the passport in the floorboards of the Volkswagen Tony drove it through the checkpoint using his own Maltese passport which, as we had already discovered, aroused no comment. Depositing the car with Pavel he returned an hour later on foot. So far so good.

Again the waiting, and the doubts. Would some smart alec recognise the car or the driver? I had passed through the checkpoint a dozen times within forty-eight hours. Twice the car had stalled, and its exhaust pipe, being punctured, caused a sensational racket. But if the car was becoming a familiar sight, would a different driver be noticed? And Pavel? Would he be recognised by one of the many policemen who had seen him under interrogation two nights previously?

Pavel was to spend the evening washing the car. He took it to some quiet spot off the Ljubljana road and scraped off the layers of thick yellow dust. A clean car was a less conspicuous car. It could also be a form of disguise. He carefully adjusted the engine speed ensuring that it raced even when idling. This was necessary for the fulfilment of his emergency instructions. Tony and I were thinking of them too as we moved up to the Italian barrier.

If Pavel, waiting in his car, was recognised he was to put his foot down hard on the accelerator and crash the border. Tony would yell a warning to the Italian officials, and I was to place myself directly in the line of fire. I did not think they would shoot. I had pathetic faith in International Tourist Year.

It was five to ten. Five minutes to "zero hour". A reluctant darkness had descended but the checkpoints, fifty yards apart, were bathed in garish light. The minutes crawled by. I watched one, two, three cars come through. Then a gap. Only one Yugoslav official was on passport duty but two others hung around. A machine gun slit in a concrete blockhouse leered at me. Another car came into the yellow sphere of light fifty yards away. Ten o'clock. The car passed through. Tony and I moved close up against the Italian Customs house. The palms of my hands were sticky and my mouth was dry.

Suddenly, like the star-turn in a cabaret, Pavel's car was transfixed in the yellow spotlight. I watched him hand the passport to the Yugoslav. The man flipped through the pages, glanced at the driver, then spoke. I saw Pavel nod. A moment of eternity as nothing happened. My body twitched as the passport was handed back with a brief salute. The car leapt forward—and stalled. In an agony I heard the starter whirr and the engine catch. The Yugoslav turned at the high-pitched screech of the punctured exhaust, but the car was at the Italian barrier. I hardly saw the brief formalities repeated. It didn't matter anymore. Pavel was free.

CHAPTER 19

Italian Caprice

In those ecstatic moments, when the three of us stood transfixed with wonderment and triumph, we all learnt the meaning of that most maligned of words—freedom. Pavel perhaps most of all, but Tony and I were also to feel its priceless heritage as the cars came trickling past the barriers, unaware of the drama they had witnessed.

But freedom is a fragile commodity. It has to be nourished and kept alive with infinite care and guarded with passionate devotion.

For Pavel it nearly founded in a web of bureaucracy spun by the very guardians of this liberty.

Trieste lay at our feet, a fairy city of flickering illumination pulsating in the darkness. Where the city ended the sea began and the moon had unrolled upon its millpond surface a staircarpet of light that ended in the semi-circle of the harbour.

It was a sight to stir the blood and I glanced sharply at Pavel to see the reaction of a man who was looking upon the free world for the first time in twenty years.

He said "Nice, isn't it," but his eyes put it more eloquently. Tony started the car again and as the three of us wound down the hill behind the city the magic disintegrated into a modern urban slum.

Before we retired to bed the extravagance of a Scotch and soda seemed appropriate but the fatigue of three sleepless nights defeated any gaiety. To get Pavel into a hotel we had to resort to the ruse of the forged passport which had won for him so recently his freedom. It seemed now, within the security of a true democracy, a shameful task but we were too tired to argue with officialdom.

I lay in bed that stifling night letting the waves of fatigue flow through me but sleep was elusive. The Yugoslav frontier was only seventeen kilometres away and possible retribution too close for comfort. Tomorrow, in Pavel's small Volkswagen, we would journey to Milan to give my brother-in-law his new life. I looked at my watch. It was already tomorrow. In less than three hours we would be on the road. Sleep did come however and the thunderstorm that hit Trieste in the small hours mingled with my dreams as the wrath of the gods of Communism.

I was mildly surprised to see Pavel still at large when we went to collect him before the dawn. The *patron* had been understandingly suspicious of an Englishman who spoke little English but no stern-eyed posse of police awaited us. Well I knew that we should have turned Pavel, as an illegal immigrant, over to the Italian authorities, but the urge to complete the miracle of escape was irresistible.

Like an avenging angel the storm followed us most of the way to Milan and, as we crossed the Lombardy plain, it bowled over tree after tree from the long straight avenues to block our path. But the treeless *autostrada* rescued us and by midday we were sweating in the sun-blistered city. But Milan was not to be the gateway to Pavel's final freedom. The British Consul and his visa officer were polite, even sympathetic, but diplomacy knows no short-cuts. Freedom was by way of the refugee camps and the ponderous machinery of Italian law. We held a conference in the cathedral, partook of a snack in the nearest restaurant and ditching the car, caught the night train to Rome. Italian law was not going to be obliged without a struggle.

To obtain accommodation at short notice in an inexpensive Rome hotel it is necessary to know the ropes. We know the ropes now but it cost us dear in shoe leather and, later, lire. Once more the problem of the passportless Pavel faced us. The *patron's* hand kept hovering over the telephone as we fibbed our way through a not too plausible explanation. He was persuaded from ringing the police but Pavel still didn't get his room. Shelving the problem we located the British Embassy.

The visa clerk, a damsel of great severity, accepted our story as if British-sponsored Iron Curtain escapees were a daily phenomenon. The visa officer, when at last we could see him, read us the riot act and we were debating the chances of obtaining political asylum for Pavel in the Vatican when a good Samaritan, in the guise of the First Secretary, descended upon us.

The fact that our tame refugee had not only eluded Yugoslav border guards but also the Italian State Police all the way from Trieste to the Eternal City was something for the book. Yes, they would send telegrams to London. Yes, he would fix the police. No promises, mind you, but ——. Confidence simply oozed out of our champion of liberty.

And he was as good as his word. That night Pavel and I were installed, as unregistered guests, in the most comfortable of hotels close by the Colosseum. Tony had to remain in the original pension since it was only a police order that got us the room.

150

The British Embassy had been given five days to work the oracle and get Pavel out of Italy after which, if it failed, Italian law would claim its victim. We thought this a very sporting offer and feeling like competitors in a game of Ludo got to work on the dice. First man home was the winner and Pavel's freedom the prize.

First forfeit went to us upon discovery that the Italian ultimatum included the week-end thus reducing our five working days to three. Commandeering the hotel telephone exchange I reinforced the Embassy telegram with some of my own to as many influential acquaintances I could rake up. Here we were debited with another forfeit when it was discovered that my prize asset—Fenner Brockway who would have set fire to the House of Lords for us—had taken to his sickbed. But I scored a point by ringing my father and arranging for Marie, safely in England, to seek political asylum without further delay thus adding strength to our arm.

A major proportion of our three working days was spent in the Embassy where Pavel was closely questioned on every aspect of his life and times. We also tracked down a lady member of the Indonesian Embassy who, as well as being a distant relative of Pavel had, it was reputed, more intimate connections with President Soekarno. How this would help us was not clear but to leave no stone unturned seemed logical. Over the week-end and in the evenings we became tourists. When in Rome—and all that. The Colosseum, St. Peter's and the Vatican, the Palatino, the Pantheon, all were subjected to our gaze but, no doubt, they will survive another thousand years. Even an attempt was made to see the exiled Archbishop of Prague, Mgr. Beran, since even spiritual help was not to be ignored. The heat of Sunday drove us to the sea at Ostia but the black sand and brown water of the Rome Lido gave us little satisfaction while the restricted and crowded beaches made bank holiday Blackpool look a rural retreat.

Monday came and, with it, the axe fell. The cable from London said "No" in almost that number of words. Bureaucracy was not to be robbed of its machinations. For us defeat was bitter but, after all, it only meant delay. That afternoon Tony flew home from Fiumicino airport and the following morning, Cinderella-like, the police came for Pavel. His golden coach had turned into a black maria.

Three plain-clothes men were deemed necessary to effect the "arrest" and the hotel manager's office was unceremoniously emptied of its usual occupants as a preliminary interrogation got under way. With much arm-waving, jovial shouting and back-slapping they managed to get down Pavel's full name with only two spelling mistakes but came to grief on the Italian version of Czechoslovakia. Thereafter it was thought prudent to continue the game in the privacy of the Central Police Station and I was abruptly alone.

Late in the afternoon I was able to join Pavel and even managed a difficult interview with the department Chief of Police but could obtain no information as to his immediate future. I saw Pavel for the last time at the railway station that night. With an escort of *carabinieri* he was en route to Trieste, right back where we had started from. The pill was bitter indeed. It could have been anywhere in Italy. But Trieste...

I was catching a later train back to Milan and so was able to see him off. He had most of my money and a railway ticket to Dover. My last words were "See you in England inside of a fortnight". And I meant it.

At least I had retained my optimism.

Miraculously no fate had overtaken the car during our absence and beyond such minor irritations resulting from the deficiency of a horn, brake lights, speedometer and petrol gauge—the last named allowing the car to run out of petrol in an *autostrada* toll-booth—the journey over the Simplon to Calais was singularly uneventful. Only at Dover did things start humming again; Her Majesty's Customs impounding the car leaving me to cover the last 100 miles home on 3/8d. !

Allowing myself a day's recuperation at the office to catch up on a fortnight's work I went into action against the Home Office. An urgent appointment was made for me to undergo an interrogation by MI 5. But, alas, the name, like the Old Scotland Yard, was no more, so any latest inquisitors were undramatically, nameless Home Office security people. However I was pleased to note that my file had survived the transition and was nicely plump with the misdeeds of earlier days. The session lasted two hours and every detail of the operation involving Pavel's escape was gently squeezed out of me.

I emerged into busy Holborn a very subdued man. An assortment of emotions spun through my mind. Incredulity that one small refugee electronics engineer could occupy the attentions of so many civil servants, dismay that their investigation was going to take "at least six weeks", despair that they almost had me believing that Pavel was a spy. Their reasoning for this startling accusation was simple. With his wife in the West and Pavel an automatic hostage to ensure her safe return he should have been under police surveillance. Yet how had he managed to leave Czechoslovakia? And again when we had both been arrested for suspicious loitering in a forbidden border zone in Yugoslavia why had they let us both go? I saw their point. But I also knew Pavel.

In the best traditions no M.P. would touch the matter while "security" had its claws in it. Unwritten names like Burgess, Maclean, Blake and Kroeger shone dimly through our correspondence. Fenner Brockway, fully recovered and back in the Labour benches, was pressed into service as well as the new Conservative member for my constituency, Peter Kirk, so it was a two-party affair. I couldn't find a Liberal.

For six weeks, with occasional promptings, I waited. The promptings increased from the first day of the seventh week and about three weeks later one barrier collapsed. The first news came through Fenner Brockway in a letter signed by the Home Secretary. It came again a few days later in an identical letter through Peter Kirk signed by the Secretary of State. A week later the same letter came direct to me signed by a clerk. They seem short of carbon paper at the Home Office. But the letters all said that Pavel would be allowed to enter the country on a work permit.

My troubles are over I thought. Work permits are a dime a dozen. Through my firm I had got several Pakistanis into the country with no bother at all. I applied on form No. ARI/9760(S4) and waited. It came straight back from the local labour office marked in red ink. No go. I rephrased the application choosing words as carefully as ever William Shakespeare did for a sonnet. True, our firm had not the slightest use for an electronic engineer but I had soon discovered one. In fact, the future of the firm was dependent upon the services of an electronic engineer. The local manager was most helpful. What sort of computor was Pavel going to operate? What kind of low voltage phasing was to be introduced? I surrendered. I even told the truth. But I was damned from the start. Our firm was on short time.

I tried fresh tactics. I contacted three electronic firms in the district. Three directors were interested, three directors said they might be willing to employ Pavel but three directors declined to apply for a work permit until they had interviewed him. I was back in square one.

Fearing for my sanity I wrote straight to the Minister of Labour himself. Maybe working downward from the top would produce results. Too true it did. Next day the chief of the foreign labour division rang up. Maybe we could arrange for the Home Office to allow your brother-in-law in on a different type of visa, he suggested. It would take a few weeks but—. The chap was trying anyway. Then my local manager friend rang up. He sounded breathless. "Your brother-in-law's file is here," he said, "it's got "minister's case" on it and it's signed by two of 'em! I'm sending it straight to head office with my recommendations."

For the first time for a long time I relaxed. I could even smile. The picture of Pavel's red-hot file whistling round the corridors of power struck me as comical.

The work permit arrived a couple of days later. I was tempted to frame it but, instead, express-posted it to Pavel now in Naples.

Two weeks passed. The silence was disturbing. I sent two telegrams and rang the embassy in Rome. "Everything's going fine," said the first secretary with enthusiasm. "The visa's granted and it's just a case of the Italian exit visa. You wouldn't believe how long-winded some governmental authorities can be." I thought that I could.

Christmas was a week ahead. I contemplated spending it in Naples. And then came a telephone call that told us Pavel was on his way. Our informant was none other than the exiled Archbishop of Prague. Our efforts to gain spiritual help had not been in vain.

I met Pavel at Dover on a damp afternoon. We greeted one another in the cold English fashion but a celebration cognac seemed appropriate. "You'll have to wait seven minutes till opening time," said the landlord.

Pavel, too, had reached freedom.

EPILOGUE

Pavel and Marie were still not to escape retribution but the price for their freedom remained a bargain. Each was awarded a prison sentence *absente reo* and their property confiscated by the state. Nor did I get off scott-free, my crime being labelled "aiding and abetting".

But they were the convulsions of a dying regime.

In the first months of 1968 strange events began occurring in Czechoslovakia. Already the voice of liberty was whispering but with the deposition of the Stalinist President Novotny a wave of liberalisation swept through a country that had borne the oppressive weight of Communism for twenty years. The voice became a bellow.

As the trappings of a police state were shouldered off by a joyous populace the growls of displeasure from Soviet Russia in the east and her satellite empire in the north and south increased in volume. The meetings and treaty-makings of Cierna-nad-Tisou and Bratislava gave the new Czech leader, Alexander Dubcek, breathing space but little peace of mind. The threat remained.

There are those who said at this time that Anna and I could have waited—even though it would have meant the loss of eleven years of happy married life. Others, more pertinently, suggested that Pavel and Marie would have been let out if they, too, had waited just a few months. Anyone can be clever after the event but even at its height the new liberalisation did not progress that far.

Then on the 21st August the Soviet Army occupied the country and Czechoslovakia stood on the threshold of a new dark age.

While the citizens of Prague demonstrated their violent disapproval in a manner little short of open revolution I called at the Czechoslovak Embassy in London. I collected an entry visa in eight minutes flat. The few shillings expended upon it was worth every penny if only for the novel experience of acquiring a Communist visa with such astonishing ease.

However my reasoning went deeper than that.

For four of its characters the fairy-tale ending of the story has prevailed. But though the Russian tanks have lumbered out of sight the fate of a nation stands in the balance. Re-enslavement or open warfare will tip the scales. One small Englishman, however deeply he feels himself involved in the destiny of one small country, can do little to help in either circumstance. But if it's to be a fight they can count him in. It would at least be a gesture. And one small Englishman has some accounts to settle of his own.

INDEX

Vlasta, 15, 16.
Vltava River, 78.
Vogliano, 139, 141.
Volkswagen, 138, 141, 147-149.
Vopo, 121.

W

War Office, 90, 111.
Warsaw, 113, 115, 116.
Westminster, 110, 125.
Wiener Neustadt, 38.
Wolseley, 8 hp., 31, 39.
Wroclaw, 115.
Wuerzburg, 19.

Y

Yugoslavia—Army, 36; border, 36, 149; car admired in, 115; cheese, 37; 1953, 31; official, 148; Partisans, 139, 140; Pavel to, 137; people from, 9; petrol, 32, 34; prisoners, 11; Travel agency, 32; walk into, 146.

Z

Zabrze see Hindenburg.
Zadar, 34.
Zagreb, 31, 36, 44, 45.
Zakopane, 108, 115, 116.
Zapotocky, President Antonin, 83-85.
Zenk, Herr, 38, 96.